C000160573

SOC

MEDIA FOR

BEGINNERS

THE COMPLETE GUIDE TO LEARN SOCIAL MEDIA MARKETING

Table of Contents

This document is geared towards providing exact and reliable information with regards to the topic and issue covered. The publication is sold with the idea that the publisher is not required to render accounting, officially permitted, or otherwise, qualified services. If advice is necessary, legal or professional, a practiced individual in the profession should be ordered.

- From a Declaration of Principles which was accepted and approved equally by a Committee of the American Bar Association and a Committee of Publishers and Associations.

themselves, not affiliated with this document.

WELCOME TO THE GUIDE TO SOCIAL MEDIA!

Welcome to Guide to Social Media! Regardless of whether you're new to social media or merely hoping to close a couple of information holes, we're happy you halted by. At this point, we've all heard how significant even social media can be. Regardless of whether your modern slant inclines more toward excitement or anxiety, it is doubtful around the way that web-based social networking is an unquestionably more unpredictable field than it initially appears. Making a plunge without a sense for what it can be overpowering and fabricating a system that gives genuine worth takes both sharp and challenging work; however, dread not—we're here to help! We trust you'll see this as one of the complete social media assets accessible, and that regardless of what your expertise level is, there's bounty here to assist you with improving your social nearness. What are we hanging tight for? We should make a plunge!

What is Social media?

"Social media" is a route for individuals to convey and connect on the web. While it has been around since the beginning of the World Wide Web, over the most recent ten years or so, we've seen a flood in both the number and ubiquity of social media destinations. It's called social media since clients draw in with (and around) it in a social setting, which can incorporate discussions, discourse, and other client produced comments and commitment communications.

Distributing content has gotten exponentially less complicated in the course of the most recent quite a while, which has helped soar the utilization of social media. Non-specialized web clients are currently ready to effortlessly make content on a quickly developing number of stages, including those that are possessed (facilitated networks, online journals, and so forth.), leased (interpersonal organizations or outsider networks), and involved (remarking, contributing, and so on.). The present web has moved from a "one-to-many" to a "many-to-many" technique for commitment, and we're cherishing it.

For organizations, the move in web commercialization and going with ascend in social media brings both fate and duty. The sheer measure of information that clients make accessible through social media alone has web advertisers hoping for happiness. The genuine enchantment, be that as it may, lies in the chance to develop enduring and versatile associations with your association's client base through web-based social networking. This is additionally where your online duty to your clients starts to come to fruition. Similarly, as your clients' conduct has moved, so have their desires for yours. Regardless of whether your business is tuning in and connecting with or not, clients are having discussions significant to your activities. It's smarter to be a piece of the debate, isn't that so? We sure think so!

Is social media only a prevailing fashion?

In the course of the most recent quite a long while, there has been a blast of development in well known online networking stages like Facebook, Twitter, Google+, LinkedIn, YouTube, Pinterest, and numerous others. It's sheltered to state that the time of web-based social networking is merely beginning, and the requirement for social media in business will just get more grounded after some time. The entire world has seen the effect of the development and selection of social media strategies, and the rising details represent themselves.

REASONS WHY SOCIAL MEDIA IS NOT A FAD

What does a business requirement for development? The appropriate response is necessary, effective promoting that prompts worldwide item introduction, increment in rush hour gridlock, commitment with existing clients, arriving at new clients, and very much refreshing picture of organization culture and greatness. To accomplish all these in the present advanced world, the unspoiled reach redistributes online networking. Presently, when internet-based life assumes such a massive job in developing economies, then how it very well may be a craze? Unquestionably not! Social media is staying put and form better with time. Right now, we examine six reasons why internet based life is beyond what a prevailing fashion and how associations can use it for their development and extension.

Amplifies Product Visibility: These days, purchasers are congregating via web-based networking media expansively; hence advertisers need to take their items or administrations where the clients are! To discover any data or arrangement, the principal thing clients do is to connect with the individuals in their systems on the distinctive social media accounts. Simultaneously on the off chance that they run over the item or administration on the web, at that point, they make the buy seeing the visuals and perusing the substance. Plus, they will, in general, be increasingly responsive to visuals and material showed via web-based networking media than the conventional techniques that help in future deals as well. Henceforth it is essential to amplify item permeability to drive sales, which are best accomplished by online networking.

A few people feel the fame of internet-based life systems would blur the following two or three years! Indeed, it may occur, however when one informal community loses the notoriety, at that point, another system comes up forcefully. As the objective clients switch their internet based life accounts, advertisers also need to proceed onward and adjust to the changes.

Irrespective of the adjustment in the system's prominence, social media holds the advantage in advertising since viewership on TV and customary media is consistently diminishing, and purchasers invest more energy in portable than in the physical stores or markets. For instance, in 2005,MySpace was well known, while in 2019,Instagram is most sought after; in this manner, advertisers are having engaging posts of their items on Instagram. Likewise, applications are increasing more adequacy for web-based shopping than the stores, so advertisers are arriving at the objective clients with the issues on web-based shopping applications, consequently, regardless of whether informal communities change. However,social media would keep on being an extraordinary advertising apparatus for amplifying item perceivability.

Invigorates Global Reach: Existing clients are the advantage for the organization, and yet it is likewise imperative to have new clients for business development and extension. The expansion to the deals happens when the clients in new areas are distinguished and connected by the organization. Also, internet-based life is pressed with chances to arrive at new objective clients in any field, city, state, or nation. Advertisers must use this, however much as could be expected.

Furthermore, the essential need for life prior was nourishment, garments, and haven; however, now it has heartily included digital screens as individuals everywhere throughout the world are snared to their screens – to be specific cell phones, tablets, or note pads. To contact them face to face in each nook and corner of the globe is merely unrealistic; however, with social media, it is particularly conceivable. Moreover, online networking invigorates to fabricate solid ties with would-be clients by drawing in them in different conversations occurring around the brand. It is amazingly vital for any business to arrive at the intended interest group and have an immediate association with them. Also, most of the shoppers react promptly via web-based networking media stages. In this manner, to arrive at the global objective crowd,social media is a perfect way out.

Encourages to Gain Marketplace Intelligence: With the progression of time, social media has been growing plentifully not exclusively to arrive at the intended interest group yet,also help gain commercial center insight. The information gathered from social media investigation is chaotic, yet it empowers to comprehend the market, know customer conduct,and screen rivalry profoundly.

• Market Understanding: The information acquired from social media helps to spot new patterns to drive item advancement, discover which item sells in a particular market, right sort of informing to improve introduction and deals of the article, and so forth. Using this information to business knowledge, advertisers can grasp the market thoroughly to distinguish the chances and dangers winning at some random time.

• Consumer Behavior: Social media offers a

profound understanding of buying conduct and examples of target shoppers in an online situation, for example, what sort of items and administrations they purchase, what they feel about the issues, etc. Right now, plotting buyer information from internet-based life, associations can have a superior understanding of clients and possibilities.

• Monitor Competition: Market is serious where various brands are dashing against each other to win a similar client subsequently through web-based social networking, associations can discover the edge in the opposition by investigating continuous information on the number of perspectives on different posts, estimating effort achievement, administering commitment around item dispatches, and so forth. It empowers advertisers to upgrade the ongoing efforts just as grow progressively engaged procedures to heighten the scope to the intended interest group.

Picking up commercial center knowledge through social media guarantees the potential piece of the overall industry is tapped effectively and never lost to the contenders.

Forces Strategic Business Partnerships:

Life is increasingly vital with between reliance. In this manner, it bodes well to have it in business as well. Deliberately working with other industry empowers both the organizations occupied with an association to arrive at the worldwide market and achieve enormous advantages. Online networking assumes an indispensable job to accomplish the elite from the vital business association, a ground-breaking severe apparatus to approach the new market, extending the objective client base, and start to lead the pack in the opposition.

On the planet that is getting progressively mind-boggling because of the rise of new advancements and market vulnerabilities consistently, it is perfect for confronting it alongside the different businesses. What's more, to do as such, online networking is the best stage to scan for these new vital business associations and run the co-advertising effort as one to contact a vast worldwide crowd.

• Search Companies for Strategic Business Partnership: The majority of times, two organizations go into the synergistic consent to accomplish the shared objectives by sharing the assets anyway. On occasion, there are multiple organizations, too, in such vital business associations. To discover such organizations for the essential business unit is a great deal troublesome than said!

To encourage this inquiry of distinguishing the organization whose administrations or item supplements yours, it is ideal to utilize social media stages providing food B2B section, for example, LinkedIn. To remain concentrated on the hunt via web-based networking media, clarify the target and framework as what kind of organization you are searching for a critical business association. Later utilize the catchphrases to have an increasingly specific inquiry.

• **Co-marking Marketing Campaigns**: Marketing advancement crusade driven by at least two organizations that are not contenders but instead need to arrive at a similar objective crowd is viewed as a silver projectile, and it turns pivotal when it is run via web-based networking media.

Whenever done right, the final product increments in devotees, sees likes, visits on the site, and more significant commitment with the intended interest group. Co-marking showcasing efforts are one in addition to one equivalents eleven. This occurs so because the co-marking advertising efforts offer the substance before the online crowd with a distinction that catches their eye and produces discussions unexpectedly. Hereafter, to exploit noticeable brand quality and nearness amid target crowd to drive deals, decide on vital business association inspired by internet-based life from the beginning (looking through the accomplices) till the end (co-marking showcasing efforts). Try not to neglect this chance!

Transform Customers into Brand Advocates: An upbeat client is a key to the accomplishment of any business, and when they usually transform into a true fan supporting different purchasers about the organization's item and administrations, then unquestionably the development is ensured. Nowadays, as more often than not, customers are on the web, they share their encounters and suppositions via web-based networking media. If there should arise an occurrence of some dropout, the advertisers can react instantly to the client's interests and resolve it at all conceivable time. Therefore, advertisers would win client steadfastness, and item's market situating is reinforced.

Also, if the clients are happy with the

administrations or item quality, they are glad to like pages and leave positive remarks. Once in awhile, the item or administration video conveying some social message gets an enormous reaction and turns into a web sensation. A viral video is a significant stake for the associations as it makes a long haul position for the brand, and it remains with the watchers for a broad timeframe. Likewise, it is, to a great extent,useful for brand advancement just as supportive in creating a one of a kind character of the organization amid the worldwide crowd. In an ongoing study, 69% of advertisers discovered internet based life incredibly valuable for building an unwavering fan base.

Recoveries the Resources: Marketing consumption is one of the significant expenses to the organization, and among all the choices accessible, the advertisers see costs brought about via web-based networking media as least when contrasted with all other showcasing channels. Why not? After every single social medium has limited the world and changed how individuals associate with each other. Subsequently, with fewer costs and more deals, social media empowers the association to achieve money related or different business objectives. Like this, advertisers are offering outstanding quality to online networking in their showcasing and deals spending plans. Time and cash are the two significant assets of each association for advertising and sales. Both are spared tremendously through internet-based life. Let us expand it further.'

Ten years prior, to contact the worldwide crowd for some commitment for items and administrations unquestionably would have been soaring costly considering voyaging and different costs; however, now it is conceivable to arrive at a similar objective crowd sitting in the workplace. Furthermore, with the correct informing and visuals, associations can fuel client commitment around the world at least expense.Mainly, online networking saves a ton on schedule, and cash spent to dispatch, run, and screen the advertising efforts. How it got conceivable? We as a whole know, the answer is social media.

Internet-based life likewise spares the assets by empowering to all the more likely comprehend the client and contenders as it drives tuning in, planning, drawing in, and at last direct traffic back to associations' claimed channels, specifically site and online store to the previous activity 'deals transformation'. Grouping everything, it is apparent that online networking spares a lot of assets of associations to draw in new clients, holding old clients, and creating more income for the organizations.

Last Thoughts: Social media is an instrument that can be utilized imaginatively in numerous manners for an association. Labeling it as a prevailing fashion will be a severe mix-up! Over 90% of advertisers all through the world have cited internet based life as 'generally significant' for their authoritative development. It would not have occurred if social media was brief or was declining on the development diagram. The check of dynamic clients on the web and advertisers utilizing social media is expanding each day, so don't be forgotten about considering 'uncertainties' and 'buts'! Instead, contribute the endeavors to investigate the online networking profoundly, associate with your intended interest group, and grow your business.

For what reason does my organization need social media?

Regardless of whether you are running a little, nearby activity, or heading a worldwide endeavor level exertion, the insights above make it understood: Your clients are on the web. They are associating in social channels with their companions, partners, and different brands looking for data, suggestions, and diversion. If your organization isn't around to reply, a contender will be. In doing as such, your rival will very likely remove the current client, alongside any other individual tuning in.

There are vast amounts of chances to include esteem—even to enjoyment!— and making that association can help manufacture an individual's relationship with an organization, brand, or agent. Those connections make the establishment for what can, in the end, become one of your most unique promoting resources: client support. Since such a large amount of the client experience currently lives on the web, internet-based life empowers brands to participate in a client's online encounter outside of the normalchannels.

If you ever end up stuck a dilemma, your backers will help the rest to remember the world that they're pulling for. Support isn't something that you can discover or purchase. Promotion is earned after some time through consistent and positive commitment with your client base. It is made through encounters that please, and through the conveyance of the most noteworthy class of client assistance. The backing is the nirvana of social media, and it is through support that your endeavors start to scale and develop genuinely. It shows that your image is doing such a stunning activity, that your clients yell about your image from housetops, imparting their insights and encounters with their systems. That sharing is the best promoting a brand can request.

Recognizing potential supporters is a decent initial step. You can utilize social devices (vast numbers of which are sketched out in the remainder of this guide), site information, client information, and even your perceptions to assist you with selecting which clients are probably going to step up to the plate bat for your image. You'll need to make sense of what is generally critical to those potential promoters. What are they searching for? It is safe to say that they are angling for acknowledgment? Is it safe to say that they are energized by select access to news or potentially content? Make sense of what kind of supporters your image pulls in and discover approaches to remember them for their promotion. It is essential to note, however, that the majority of your most noteworthy network connections will be fabricated naturally. While your examination and brand information supports individuals and causes you to put the correct foot forward, relationships require some investment.

The progress from a latent web to an intuitive network has carried with it numerous progressions influencing how people associate with each other and how organizations work. At this phase in the game, most would agree that a web nearness is essential to the achievement of a business. You can't excel in case you're disregarding your client's online discussions or selecting to look the other way. Utilize this chance to draw nearer to your crowd than at any additional time—contact more individuals in a certifiable and bona fide way, drive progressively qualified site traffic, increment the authority of your image, connect with the individuals who impact your clients' conduct, and increase the information necessary for bits of knowledge-based business choices. Perhaps a superior inquiry is, the reason wouldn't your organization utilize online networking?

By what means would social be able to be a springboard for achievement in other advertising channels?

Remember that neither your clients' experience nor your image begins with Twitter, Facebook, or your blog. Internet-based life should take your current model and set it, electrify it, and reinforce it. Your endeavors in online networking ought to be an expansion of everything else you do in all branches of your organization. Catching your organization's voice and offering it to the world through social media will open up one of a kind open doors in every single other channel of inbound promoting, including SEO, marking, advertising, deals, and then some.

Connections

To take advantage of social media, make the connections you work with it your ultimate objective. That may sound somewhat idealistic for any individual who is grounded in progressively conventional and unmistakable business estimation and measurements, however, make a stride once again from the primary concern, ROI-chasing angle to take a gander at the 10,000-foot view for a moment. The connections worked with clients are the establishments after that different parts of your business can and will thrive. Connections thrive when you develop them, and no other region offers you the chance to do this just as social media. Social channels have separated the dividers between people at an exceptional rate. By and large, 3.74 degrees of partition away from each other, making them almost as associated with one another as Kevin Bacon is to the remainder of Hollywood. In the years since that review, the system has just kept on developing. That is truly stunning, and social media can assume praise for getting it going.

The absolute best SEOs and advertising experts gain their reputation, at any rate, to some extent, from the connections they can construct. They're additionally acceptable at what they do; obviously, however, extraordinary relationships support their adequately intense exertion. The links you work with your clients lead to promotion and dedication, characteristics that can bolster your image during both the great and the terrible occasions, speaking to speculation that will stay solid on about any stage and under almost any conditions.

Input

Data can be shared through online networking at an incredibly quick pace, and clients are progressively going to social diverts to share data continuously. This data regularly appears as feelings, so in case you're tuning in for the correct prompts from your crowd, web-based social networking can turn into a priceless wellspring of experiences and criticism. Consolidating social tuning in into item advancement work can go about as an initial notice framework, save money on client care costs, give valuable improvement input, and even assistance recognize perfect beta analyzers absent a lot of expenses.

Combination

Web-based social networking isn't something you can just "attach" to the remainder of your promoting, marking, PR, and publicizing endeavors; it should be anutterly coordinated piece of the blend. In doing such, you can make a secure and versatile experience for your clients. Consider it an unfortunate obligation, and not an end in itself. Additionally, it's not as hard as it sounds. Make sure to incorporate internet based life into your promoting endeavors as right on time as conceivable to help enhance and harden your work instead of holding up until the finish of an arranging cycle to investigate social alternatives. If a social nearness is evident from the beginning, your marking will profit by extra client touchpoints, PR will see a lift in impressions and reach, and client assistance can proactively tune in and actuate where fundamental. As should be obvious, social nearness can have an expansive effect on your association when it is executed genuinely and insightfully. By making the social commitment a centerpiece of your tasks instead of an idea in retrospect, you have superior taken shots at completely utilizing its capacity.

TYPES OF SOCIAL MEDIA AND HOW EACH CAN BENEFIT YOU

As a web-based social networking genius, you most likely as of now utilize all the most significant informal organizations (Facebook, Twitter, LinkedIn) and media sharing locales (Instagram, YouTube, Snapchat), alongside possibly a bunch of others like Pinterest and Google Plus. In any case, there's significantly more to web-based life than the top web-based life and media sharing systems. Look past those web-based social networking juggernauts, and you'll see that individuals are utilizing a wide range of sorts of internet-based life to associate online for a wide range of reasons.

In our mission to present to you the most recent and best web-based life news from all sides of the web, we've discovered a lot of hyper-centered specialty interpersonal organizations for everything from fly setting and green living to weaving and everything masculine. In any case, gathering informal communities as indicated by the topic rapidly gets overpowering—and once in a while, diverting. (Additionally, Wikipedia's as of now done it for us.) And keeping in mind that sometime in the past, you could necessarily order systems as indicated by their practical capacities (Twitter for short content substance, YouTube for video, etc.), that time has passed. As more systems include rich highlights like livestreaming and augmented reality, the lines between their capabilities proceed to obscure and change quicker than a great many people have the opportunity to find out about the changes.

So as opposed to classifying systems as per hyper-explicit client premiums or moving innovation highlights, we want to think like advertisers and gathering methods into ten general classifications that attention on what individuals would like to achieve by utilizing them. Here's our rundown of 10 sorts of internet-based life and what they're used for:

• Social systems—Connect with individuals

• Media sharing systems—Share photographs, recordings, and other media

• Discussion discussions—Share news and thoughts

• Bookmarking and substance curation systems—Discover, spare, and offer new substance

• Consumer survey systems—Find and audit organizations

• Blogging and distributing policies—Publish content on the web

• Interest-based systems—Share interests and leisure activities

• Social shopping systems—Shop on the web

• Sharing economy systems—Trade merchandise and ventures

• Anonymous informal organizations—Communicate namelessly

Thinking about these classes of online networking and understanding why individuals use them can open up new thoughts and channels for connecting with your crowd all the more adequately—so how about we begin..

1. Interpersonal Relationship

Models: Facebook, Twitter, LinkedIn

Why individuals utilize these systems: To interface with individuals (and brands) on the web.

How they can profit your business: Let us check the ways: statistical surveying, brand mindfulness, lead age, relationship building, client support.The rundown is virtually constant. Interpersonal organizations, once in a while called "relationship systems," help individuals and associations interface online to share data and thoughts. While these systems aren't the most established kind of web-based life, they inevitably characterize it now. These channels began as generally essential administrations—for instance, Twitter was the spot to respond to the inquiry "what's going on with you?" and Facebook was the place you may check the relationship status of that adorable Economics 101 cohort.

Presently, and particularly since the ascent of the versatile web, these systems have become center points that change almost every part of current life—from perusing news to sharing excursion photographs to getting another line of work—into a social encounter. In case you're not utilizing these center systems yet as a component of your web-based life advertising plan—or in case you're searching for thoughts to improve your current methodology—you'll discover an abundance of usable data in our advisers for Facebook, Twitter, and LinkedIn.

2. Media sharing systems

Models: Instagram, Snapchat, YouTube

Why individuals utilize these systems: To discover and share photographs, video, live video, and other media on the web. How they can profit your business: As the significant relationship arranges, these destinations are priceless for brand mindfulness, lead age, crowd commitment, and a large portion of your other social promoting objectives. Media sharing systems give individuals and brands a spot to discover and share media web-based, including photographs, video, and live video.

The lines between media sharing systems and informal communities are obscuring nowadays as social relationship systems like Facebook and Twitter include live video, increased reality, and other sight and sound administrations to their foundation. Nonetheless, what recognizes media sharing systems is that the sharing of media is their characterizing and essential role. While most of the posts on relationship systems contain content, posts on networks like Instagram and Snapchat start with a picture or video, to which clients may choose to include content like inscriptions, notices of different clients, or channels that make you resemble a rabbit. Thus, on destinations, for example, YouTube and Vimeo, video is the essential method of correspondence.

While deciding if your business needs to build up a nearness on a media sharing system, it's essential to think about your accessible assets. If there's one thing the best brands on stages like YouTube or Instagram share for all intents and purpose, it's a wholly arranged crucial painstakingly planned media resources, usually following a particular subject. To build your business' odds of progress on media sharing systems, see our advisers for promoting on Instagram,Snapchat, YouTube, and Vimeo.

3. Conversation gatherings

Models: Reddit, Quora, Digg

Why individuals utilize these systems: To discover, examine, and share news, data, and conclusions.

How they can profit your business: These systems can be fantastic assets for statistical surveying. Done right, you can likewise promote them. However, you'll be mindful to keep your advertisements and posts isolated. Conversation gatherings are perhaps the most seasoned sort of web-based social networking. Before we associated with our first college companions on The Facebook, we examined mainstream society, current undertakings, and requested assistance on discussions. Investigate the broad reach and huge client numbers on gatherings, for example, Reddit, Quora, and Digg, and you'll see that the open's hunger for aggregate information and astuteness stays insatiable.

These are where individuals go to discover what everybody's discussing and say something regarding it—and clients on these locales by and large aren't timid about communicating their sentiments. While social relationship systems are progressively actualizing measures to lessen secrecy and make a sheltered space on the web, conversation discussions by and large permit clients to stay mysterious, keeping a portion of the "wild west" feel objectified to characterize the online experience. This can make conversation gatherings, for example, Reddit (the so-called "first page of the web") and Quora incredible spots to dive for sincere clients look into and severely legit conclusions. In case you're mindful to keep promotions and posts discrete, they can even be a spot to publicize—for all the subtleties, see our manual for Reddit promoting.

4. Bookmarking and substance curation systems

Models: Pinterest, Flipboard

Why individuals utilize these systems: To find, spare, share, and examine new and inclining substance and media.

How they can profit your business: These systems can be profoundly viable for driving brand mindfulness, client commitment, and site traffic. Bookmarking and substance curation systems help individuals find, spare, share, and examine the new and drifting substance and media. These systems are a hotbed of innovativeness and motivation for individuals looking for data and thoughts, and by adding them to your internet based life advertising plan, you'll open up new channels for building brand mindfulness and connecting with your crowd and clients.

Bookmarking systems like Pinterest help individuals find, spare and offer visual substance. A simple initial step for beginning with Pinterest is to make your site bookmark-accommodating. This involves streamlining features and pictures on your blog or potential place for the feeds these systems use to access and offer your substance. You ought to likewise give close consideration to the images highlighted on your webpage or blog. In essence, these are the window showcases of Pins, so you need them to be acceptable portrayals of your substance.

Content curation systems like Flipboard are like bookmarking systems, however, with attention on finding and sharing articles and other content substance. You can make your own Flipboard magazine to figure out the most captivating material on your subject of decision from outside sources, and to feature your element. Different sorts of systems are additionally including bookmarking and curation highlights. For instance, Instagram now offers highlights for clients to spare material and make their assortments. To begin arranging your procedure for bookmarking and substance curation systems, see our aides on utilizing Pinterest and Flipboard.

5. Customer review systems

Models: Yelp, Zomato, TripAdvisor

Why individuals use these systems: To discover, review, and offer data about brands, items, and administrations, just as eateries, travel goals, and that's just the beginning.

How they can profit your business: Positive reviews carry social verification to your cases. Taken care of well, you can resolve issues with troubled clients.

Shopper review systems give individuals a spot to audit brands, organizations, items, administrations, travel spots, and pretty much whatever else. Reviews are a sort of substance that increases the value of numerous sites and online administrations—consider the purchasing experience on Amazon or the experience of looking for a nearby business on Google Maps. Shopper review systems make it one stride further by building networks around the audit as a centerpiece of the worth they give. Area-based review administrations, for example, Yelp and Zomato, keep on developing as close to informal home communities embrace geolocation, and more clients decide to counsel the web alongside their companions for proposals of best feasting spots.

There are locales to review anything from lodgings and cafés to the business where you're considering going after a position—and client audits have more weight than any other time in recent memory. Indeed, as per an overview by BrightLocal, 88 percent of purchasers trust online reviews as much as an individual proposal. Your image must be able to draw in positive client reviews and handle negative ones. To do this, you can choose a client achievement colleague to address reviews on locales applicable to your business. Depend on them with responding to any inquiries or worries from customers with average or negative encounters, and check whether there is whatever should be possible on your conclusion to transform a potential spoiler into a fan. For additional on this theme, read our blog entries on the most proficient method to react to negative audits and online notoriety the executives.

6. Blogging and distributing systems

Models: WordPress, Tumblr, Medium

Why individuals utilize these systems: To

distribute, find, and remark on content on the web.

How they can profit your business: Content advertising can be a profoundly viable approach to connect with your crowd, assemble your image, and produce leads and deals.

Blogging and distributing systems give individuals and brands instruments to distribute content online in groups that support revelation, sharing, and remarking. These systems go from progressively conventional blogging stages like WordPress and Blogger to microblogging administrations like Tumblr and acute social distributing stages like Medium. On the off chance that your advancement procedure incorporates content showcasing (and on the off chance that it doesn't, you should think about it), your business can pick up permeability by keeping a blog. A blog doesn't merely help increment attention to your company and create additionally captivating substance for your social channels, for example, Facebook; it can likewise help cut out a specialty for your image as an idea head in your industry. In case you're beginning with blogging and substance showcasing, see our advisers for starting a blog, advancing your blog, content promoting methodology, and making extraordinary substance.

7. Social shopping systems

Models: Polyvore, Etsy, Fancy

Why individuals utilize these systems: To spot patterns, follow brands, share incredible finds, and make buys.

How they can profit your business: Brands can manufacture mindfulness, increment commitment, and sell items using new channels. Social shopping systems do web-based business connecting by including a social component.

Components of web-based businesses show up in numerous different kinds of informal communities—for instance, Pinterest highlights Buyable Pins, and Instagram gives invigorate apparatuses as "shop now" and "introduce now" catches. Social shopping systems make it one stride further by building their site around an engaged joining between the social experience and the shopping experience. Administrations like Etsy permit independent ventures and individual crafters to sell their items without a current physical area, and systems, for example, Polyvore total items from various retailers in a solitary online commercial center, and. Polyvore is one of the biggest social style networks on the web, and it's a genuine case of a system intended to coordinate the social involvement in the purchasing experience. The more significant part of the substance is created by clients, who pick items they like, make montages, distribute them as a set, and afterward share collections with different clients.

8. Intrigue based systems

Models: Goodreads, Houzz, Last.FM

Why individuals utilize these systems: To interface with others around a mutual intrigue or side interest.

How they can profit your business: If there's a system committed to the sort of items or administrations you give, these systems can be an incredible spot to draw in with your crowd and assemble brand mindfulness. Intrigue based systems adopt a more focused on strategy than the enormous informal communities do by concentrating exclusively on a single subject, for example, books, music, or home structure.

While there are gatherings and discussions on

different systems that are committed to these interests, concentrating exclusively on a single region of intrigue permits these systems to convey an encounter customized for the needs and needs of the individuals and networks who share that intrigue. For instance, on Houzz, home fashioners can peruse crafted by different planners, make assortments of their work, and interface with individuals searching for their administrations. Systems, for example, Last.fm (for artists and music darlings) and Goodreads (for writers and ardent perusers) likewise give an encounter planned explicitly to their specialty crowd.

If your clients and social crowd share a typical enthusiasm (for instance, in case you're a distributing house), an intrigue based system can be a decent spot to stay aware of current patterns among devotees of your industry or its items.

9. 'Sharing economy' systems

Models: Airbnb, Uber, Taskrabbit

Why individuals utilize these systems: To publicize, discover, share, purchase, sell, and exchange items and administrations between peers.

How they can profit your business: If you happen to offer the sort of items or administrations exchanged here, these systems can be another divert for acquiring company. (For instance, on the off chance that you work an overnight boardinghouse, Airbnb could assist you with discovering clients.)

"Sharing economy" systems, additionally called "community-oriented economy systems," interface individuals online to publicize, to learn, sharing, purchasing, selling, and exchanging items and administrations. And keeping in mind that you're presumably effectively acquainted with enormous name systems like Airbnb and Uber, there are a developing number of specialty systems you can use to discover a dogsitter, a parking space, a home-prepared dinner, and then some. This online model for peer trade has gotten suitable and famous as of late as individuals began believing in the web audits and feeling great utilizing them to measure the notoriety and dependability of venders and specialist co-ops. As per a report by advanced research firm Vision Critical, "The synergistic economy today works since trust can be confirmed electronically through interpersonal organizations... online life lets the collective economy run easily."

While most advertisers will discover these systems excessively explicitly focused on or prohibitive, on the off chance that you happen to give the sort of item or administration that is exchanged on a specific order, you should investigate it as another channel to create leads and deals.

Reward: Get the bit by bit internet based life system control with genius tips on the most proficient method to develop your online networking nearness.

10. Anonymous informal communities

Models: Whisper, Ask.FM, After School

Why individuals utilize these systems: To prattle, vent, snoop, and once in awhile menace.

How they can profit your business: They in all likelihood can't. Stay away.

Last—and least—are unknown interpersonal organizations. While significant informal communities are putting forth expanding attempts to consider clients responsible for their social movement, these locales go the other way and permit clients to post content namelessly. CBS New York portrayed Whisper as "the spot to go nowadays to vent, tell the truth, or companion into others' mysteries," says the site centers around "transforming admissions into the content."

These systems may seem like an enjoyment spot to let loose a little (for instance, in case you're a high schooler and need to whine about your folks, instructors, sweetheart, etc.). Be that as it may, they've been appeared to give a result free gathering to cyberbullying and have been connected to high schooler suicides. As we would like to think, unknown interpersonal organizations are a stage back toward the wild-west beginning of the web when we've taken in the significance of keeping the internet a protected spot for everybody. On the off chance that it merits saying, it deserves remaining behind.

Regardless of whether you're investigating new potential markets for your business or simply searching for new channels to interface with your clients, there are numerous sorts of online life you can utilize. Some are mainly required for any business; others are valuable for a little subset of specialty organizations, and some you should avoid totally. Whatever your needs and your objectives, it's a sure thing you'll discover what you're searching for someplace on social.

THE VALUE OF SOCIAL MEDIA
Building and connecting with a network

Maybe the best estimation of internet-based life showcasing is your capacity to cultivate and connect with a network of others. That commitment is at the core of web-based social networking, and without it, you're left with a bull horn and nobody to hear you. You have the chance to connect with clients from everywhere throughout the world—including the individuals who are directly down the road—for an immense scope. On the off chance that a present or planned client has a comment to you or about you, you currently can react right away.

Notwithstanding responsive correspondence, brands and organizations can start to construct associations with their clients past those that occur during typical exchanges. These connections are what keep clients returning, expanding both reliability and maintenance. On the off chance that those clients become supporters and increment your assertion of-mouth nearness, you'll begin seeing stunning returns.

By giving an incredible spot of commitment for your locale and helping assemble valuable, real assets for your image's specialty, you're likewise developing an expert for your image inside your industry. You'll discover your clients progressively believing what you state and coming to you for assets that can assist them with fathoming their difficulties. Hell, you may even end up helping out a rival in the space. All brands start in a dark comparative spot, and the more you give, the higher power you'll get back. An incredible model is REI, which sells outside rigging, but at the same time is a known asset for tips on climbing, snowshoeing, zombie endurance, and an entire host of different exercises that revolved around the outside.

Moving from "like" to "love" to "shield."

The sentiments of any network part toward your image can extend from disdain to reverence and past. We'll address the antagonistic emotions later on; the individuals we need to focus on currently are those we plan to move along a range from necessarily "enjoying" all of you the best approach to being happy to safeguard you and your image. The initial step is getting individuals just to like you, regardless of whether on Facebook, by listening in on others' conversations, or in any case. The individuals who love you are reliably having their desires met. This regularly feels value-based with a low degree of commitment. However, there's positively nothing amiss with that.

Like any relationship, shaping bonds that take you to the following level exceptionally relies upon the requirements of both your image and the people with whom you're connecting. You need to frame these bonds on positive encounters you have together that advantage both of you. (It is not necessarily the case that relationships can't be framed through difficulty, yet having state a positive Twitter trade around helping somebody is better than one around how your item is breaking down.) Even better if these encounters bring joy and manufacture your remarkable image voice. For instance, when Kotex began their Pinterest account, they choose 50 female clients and sent them one of a kind bundles dependent on their Pinterest sheets. Not exclusively were these ladies astonished and cheerful, yet ultimately shared about what Kotex did on their informal communities, making a course of warm emotions.

There is another level where this relationship becomes much more profound. At the point when a client gets ready to guard your image, you know you've genuinely beaten yourself. This last "readiness to safeguard" organize is brand and social nirvana, as network individuals are connecting much of the time and giving proposals, yet also rising to advocate your work and guard you against brand spoilers. You can never anticipate that your locale should deal with 100% of the client care issues or questions that emerge. They aren't entirely prepared, and it's not their occupation.

In any case, you can expect, after your underlying venture and development, that some network individuals will start to step up and help out when they can and where fitting. (This is a decent time to consider how to perceive and even prize your most dynamic members.) When that occurs, you start to see how your endeavors will begin to scale as you keep on boosting your locale commitment endeavors. It lets loose you to take a shot at different commitment, and as you may envision, a backer staying standing for a brand is unmistakably more impressive than a brand going to bat for itself. There's a degree of genuineness incorporated with that kind of distributed association that can't be found in brand-to-client communications.

It's not just about promoting

The people group commitment that internet based life manages is helpful to about all aspects of your association, from the item group to HR, and that's only the tip of the iceberg. If that wasn't already enough, getting more partners included will alleviate your burden. To kick you off, here are a couple of zones that see the most evident worth.

Content creation

By utilizing your pursuit of traffic information, on-location commitment, and social listening endeavors, your web-based social networking nearness can enable you to figure out what individuals are searching for and make content that satisfies their necessities. (Also giving you a brilliant method to share that content once it's accessible.) Topics for substance will probably fall in one of three pails:

Learn and improve

This kind of material is intended to advance your clients' undertakings or work processes. You are endeavoring to improve their lives by more completely using your item (highlight instruction, and so on.), or even by offering help. The primary objectives of this substance type are to manufacture authority, drive associations, and increment commitment.

Investigate and find

Clients needing to get imaginative and find better approaches to utilize your item are searching for this kind of substance. For this gathering, building connections will be principal; these connections will breed ideation and network.

Question and answer

This sort of substance serves to meet client assistance needs. Something has turned out badly, and clients look for an answer. This can extend from a point by point discussion string on settling a specific issue to a fundamental inquiry and answer on the best way to make an item return. Your principalobjective is to drive answers.

Additionally, don't neglect the substance that can be produced inside your locale. The client created content can be astonishing—a blessing, even! Your clients can help compose what your crowd finds fascinating, applicable, and valuable. The potential outcomes are inestimable.

Utilizing investigation instruments like SimplyMeasured, True Social Metrics, just as devices from the systems themselves, you can quantify the discussions you're having on Twitter, Facebook, Google+, and even YouTube for content creation thoughts.

The critical takeaway: Members of your locale are straightforwardly discussing what they need. To receive the rewards of that discussion, you should simply tune in. It's amazingly simple to determine significant bits of knowledge when you're glancing in the correct spots.

Client support

It's a quite common human response to grumble when something doesn't go our direction. Previously, we may just have vented our dissatisfaction with two or three companions. Presently, we go to Twitter and Facebook. A lot bigger crowd is tuning in there—one that isn't constrained by topography and can without much of a stretch intensify any grievances. As an organization, when people utilize their social channels as a method for grumbling about you, it tends to be alarming from the start. It can feel like you're being assaulted and like you have no control. In any case, these are chances to bounce in and help redress the circumstance, in any event, improving the client's involvement in your image.

Primary concern: We're ascending with the tide of our clients' desires.

Not all clients will address you straightforwardly, be that as it may, so it assists with being tuning in. Continuously make sure it's understood and simple for individuals to get in touch with you handily. It might help forestall a Twitter bluster or an annoyed

Facebook update. A few clients out there are prepared to draw in with questions, concerns, and even grumblings, and you must be there. In any case, you don't need to do only it. Recall that as you move your locale individuals into progressively significant associations with your image, they'll rise to protect you. You need to place in the muscle in advance; however, sooner or later, you'll begin seeing proof of your locale stepping in to help each other for your sake.

With some preparation and accentuation on predictable voice, social cooperation can be gotten by other client assistance situated divisions inside the organization. At the point when social commitment isn't the sole obligation of an internet-based life showcasing proficient, yet somewhat a circulated exertion across utilitarian territories of the organization, you'll have the option to all the more likely serve your clients while maintaining a productive and educated business.

Item advancement

At no other time in history have organizations had more access to clients at scale than they do now, and item improvement stands to profit by this maybe more than some other gathering.

Contribution from online networking, however, can be both a gift and a revile, as individuals don't generally know correctly what they think or need. There's a statement usually ascribed to Henry Ford, author of the Ford Motor Company, that goes, "On the off chance that I had asked the individuals what they needed, they would have said quicker ponies."

It's anything but complicated to treat all client contribution as gospel wrongly. Input is unimaginably significant, yet that being stated, you should take that criticism with regards to everything else you think about your item and your image. A couple of objections are not illustrative of your whole userbase, so the criticism you're seeing may not be indicative of reality. There are a few strategies you can utilize to ensure you're gathering quite a few advantages of this client input without relegating fake weight.

Make beta/analyzer networks: This should be possible in two or three different ways. You can clergyman a rundown of network individuals who might be generally useful—power clients from over the social web, devotee bloggers, etc.—into a gathering associated by email, a Facebook gathering, or another social instrument. You can likewise make extraordinary confined zones of your audience based networks where these force clients can chat, connect with, and organize while taking an interest in discussions you produce. This unparalleled access can fill in as an award for those network individuals, and it can prompt amazingly practical experiences for you and your image.

Tune in for your opposition: As you tune in for item criticism, you'll need to dissect estimation, pay a unique mind to specific issues, and see what the more noteworthy network says about your rivals. Discussions occurring around your opposition's items/contributions can give unlimited measures independently.

Estimation: Just as you can gather bits of knowledge about your items by filtering through your web investigation, you can increase comparable hints by watching and estimating the presentation of your social channels. Do posts around one piece often beat related posts about another? Your clients may be revealing to you something about which they like better.

HR

Internet-based life can assume a brilliant job in

HR, also: promising worker commitment, finding and interfacing with newcomers, and in any event, assisting with maintenance endeavors.

A word about administration: Depending on the way of life at your association, your HR office may need to influence any execution of social media, and paying little mind to the idea of life, getting their upfront investment is continuously a smart thought. Working with your HR experts during the improvement of your internet based life arrangements and administration can help guarantee your association is shielded from chance while engaging its representatives. Certainly, connect with them before maneuvering different workers into your endeavors; this is one territory where you'd preferably ask consent over absolution.

Past those administration contemplations, however, social media can be a momentous device for HR experts. A portion of the territories you might have the option to develop your endeavors into HR include:

Selecting

Social channels are the ideal spot to arrive at new candidates. Individuals look for employment opportunities on the web, and the chances are that some of them have just "preferred" you, so why not contact them where they're as of now investing their energy? Given its advantage, your locale will likewise be progressively well-suited to impart these openings to its systems.

Interior person to person communication

Some interpersonal organizations are intended to be utilized altogether inside an association. A few people like Yammer. Some lean toward Chatter. Hell, some even use Basecamp or Jive. Whatever enhance you pick, long-range informal communication devices utilized inside can be unbelievable for information sharing, assembling a feeling of kinship, and expanding cross-practical joint effort. Inner friendly communities can likewise be necessary for administration and arrangement mindfulness endeavors.

Professional success

Being dynamic and utterly mindful of the "hows and whats" of social media is rapidly turning into necessary expertise in the modern workforce. This expertise can't be ignored, particularly for HR experts. Internet-based life can likewise be utilized to arrange on the web and find out about inclining themes in a particular field, finding new zones of chance for the business that may incorporate specialty networks for related callings.

Internet-based life isn't something that ought to be exclusively used by any one group inside an organization. In a perfect world, the whole association is engaged with some features of the organization's internet-based life and has a profound comprehension of its clients through support. Cross-practically disseminating the social media exertion likewise guarantees the opportune individuals assume control at the ideal time.

Simultaneously, it's imperative to keep up a steady voice and marking for each part of your organization's social endeavors, so you'll need to, at any rate, make a lot of fundamental rules for everybody included.

Amazing, great. I'm an advertiser; however—what does this mean for me?

As more individuals all through your association understand the advantages they'll get from online networking; you'll be better ready to concentrate your endeavors on advertising rather than on being an assistance work area or a go-between. Furthermore, you have the additional advantage of scaling a portion of the expenses related to social commitment, and you will have different groups of individuals on your side assisting with presenting the business defense for interests in commitment advancement as opposed to grinding away alone. This is an establishment for progress.

Step by step instructions to get internet based life purchase in

As you present your defense for your image's internet-based life tries, you'll likely need to demonstrate an incentive to your initiative or customers. Fortunately, with a little investigation, the information is your ally. We should begin by building a business case that is directly for you.

You realize your association superior to pretty much anybody, so trust your gut. In case you're stressed over pushback, you can run some little scope tests to perceive how it proceeds to assemble a case for your exertion. In safe pockets—places where you can mess about and make the establishment for your business case absent a lot of hazards—work out a preliminary or two that address probably the most problems that are begging to be sent your association faces, and check whether you can't demonstrate the effect of social media in those zones. You may even seek your rivals for some genuine models. When these tests have yielded results, present your new information to whoever needs to offer the social hint off. This procedure of beginning little helps get you the authorization and trust you'll have to move in the direction of a portion of the more troublesome outcomes.

On the off chance that you have had a go at putting forth a business defense, you're despite everything being met with opposition, don't surrender. Give fabricating a shot explicit contextual analyses to add substance to your pitch, giving higher-ups a vibe for what it will in the long run resemble. On the off chance that you have an opportunity to begin little, plunging a toe in the water with an insignificant hazard, your outcomes can say a lot. When you have something new to appear, you can return to and reinforce your business case. It's challenging to contend with information.

SOCIAL MEDIA BEST PRACTICE
What sorts of contents to distribute and share

A typical (and reasonable) botch that numerous individuals make as they're jumping into social commitment is to constrain their substance to exclusive updates. This is intelligent of the conventional showcasing world in which all outbound push informing is only that, yet things have changed; presently, we assemble our advertising endeavors on trust, commitment, and network. There is, obviously, a period and spot for showcasing and individual messages, yet don't restrain yourself. Consider widening your degree apiece. This will make your substance all the more engaging and diminish the weight of creation. A few alternatives for sorts of updates may include:

Nearby content: It's quite a sure thing that if somebody is tailing you, they're keen on what you offer. It's a much more secure wager to state their inclinations don't stop there. Offer substance that is extraneously significant to your business or something, including shared interests of your crowd. For instance, on the off chance that you are a dress retailer, you could post about best in class magnificence patterns or news from a significant planner. These subjects very likely straightforwardly line up with the interests of your crowd.

Tips and deceives: Add an incentive to the discussion by sharing substance that will make your clients' lives simpler (extra focuses for tips and deceives that assist them with utilizing your items or administrations).

Reactions: Not each update needs to come from unique thoughts of yours; you can bob off the ideas that others are as of now posting. Social media depends on discussions, so bounce in and be a piece of them. You can even search for Twitter talks that apply to your image and make a plunge. (This is additionally a decent method to get your record and brand higher perceivability.)

Non-special organization data: If your organization accomplishes stunning charitable effort in your locale, don't be timid about sharing it! If there's a somewhat noteworthy appearing at the organization Halloween party, you unquestionably need to share that. Giving a sneak look into the way of life and network inside an association goes far to building connections by acculturating the brand. Online networking offers a fabulous approach to this.

Employment opportunities: Social channels can be an unbelievably productive spot to discover new abilities and announce employment opportunities. Employment searchers are progressively utilizing social media as a method for finding out about organizations and their open positions; it's a match made in Internet paradise. Get those postings out there and make sure to feature the most significant ones.

Jokes: This is a precarious one, and it's, to a greater extent, a marking question than everything else. As a matter of first importance, comprehend what your image is and what sort of character it epitomizes. On the off chance that amusingness isn't a piece of that, you may maintain a strategic distance from this kind of post. It can reverse discharge and be unimaginably cumbersome. If you are going to attempt humor, security first! Guarantee you're not unexpectedly sharing something that could be hostile by testing it among your partners, companions, or even family. Continuously decide in favor of alert with touchy subjects; a debacle can be extremely disturbing. When you've ensured the funniness is satisfactory, ensure it's exciting because a terrible joke merely is humiliating.

The most effective method to share and distribute your substance

Recurrence of updates

"How frequently do I have to refresh my record?" is a typical inquiry, and there is no set in a stone answer here—no best practice unchangeable. It relies upon your crowd, their hunger, and what you need to state. There has been some exploration on this point that can go about as a general rule in your endeavors, yet likewise, with most things, it's ideal for testing and seeing what works best for you and your crowd on every stage. One all-inclusive truth is that web-based social networking notices don't keep going long. The half-existence of a tweet, for instance, is around 18 minutes for most clients. This number isn't intended to propose you should post that regularly, but instead, comprehend that sending an update out doesn't mean it will stay noticeable for an apparent measure of time. Clients proceed onward to the next things in their newsfeeds rapidly. The takeaway here is to watch out for to what extent your clients are connecting with and sharing something. More than anything, this is characteristic of the nature of your substance.

Once more, however, everything relies upon what is proper for your association. For instance, news associations or media productions could without much of a stretch be relied upon to refresh different to-all the time. At the same time, a dress retailer would be depleted by this mood and therefore turn off clients. You certainly would prefer not to talk only for talking; if you don't have anything of significant worth to include, don't present updates just on meet a quantity. So, you should ensure your record refreshes usually enough to tempt clients to track. You need them to realize they could be passing up some great stuff on the off chance that they don't.

Commitment

Encouraging commitment as a brand comes in two flavors. The first is reacting to clients who refer to questions, critique, and so on. At the start of a network's advancement,a brand needs to be exceptionally present and dynamic, and this implies reacting to most client editorial and the entirety of their inquiries. The volume at this phase in the game ought to be genuinely sensible for most.

The second kind of commitment is what results from a reliable information-driven substance procedure. By seeing things like inquiry inquiries and social discussions, you can start to manufacture the establishment of a secure substance procedure. As you're sharing this substance all through your locale, you should gather information on how your crowd responds to it and draws in with it. Believe the entirety of this information to be input on how you're doing. You may reexamine the planning of your updates, the arrangement or sentence structure you use (are you posing inquiries, offering intense expressions, and so on.), and even the kind of media you're utilizing.

Request help: Want your locale to help or take an interest in a specific goal in mind? Here and there, it's as straightforward as inquiring. On the off chance that you've earned their loyalty by building worth and venture into the relationship, you can request overview support, item input, or whatever else you need. Possibly you need assistance supporting or sharing another program or bit of substance. You've made the relationship venture; they will regularly readily respond.

Keep it straightforward: Too numerous choices should be no alternatives. If your crowd isn't on a specific system, for what reason would you advance that sharing opportunity on your substance? On the other hand, if your principle center is B2B, you may (for instance) not have to incorporate Pinterest as a sharing alternative. Take a gander at your social crowd and coordinate your contributions with their practices.

Cross-advance for discoverability: There's nothing more terrible for a client than not having the option to locate your substance, and cross-advancement is a simple method to help shield that from occurring. Guarantee your blog is connected to your social properties. Keep the entirety of your profile names the equivalent over every social channel (use assistance like KnowEm to be proactive on this one), and cross-advance your records. What's more, (this is super-significant): Develop and sell a one of a kind offer for each file. Consider it—for what reason would a client need to or need to tail you on Twitter, on the off chance that they as of now tail you on Facebook? Ensure you give them an explanation.

Screen and tune in: Monitor social channels as habitually as possible. Use benefits that will help message pop-ups to you so you can guarantee you're not missing meaningful discussions over the web. There are many applications for Twitter and Facebook (SocialEngage, HootSuite, TweetDeck, and so on.) accessible, and you can set up alarms, too (Fresh Web Explorer, IFTTT). Regularly the administrator instruments of different stages will have this usefulness worked in. As you screen, truly tune in to what your clients let you know. Social listening information gives unlimited bits of knowledge to brands and organizations ready to tune in. This can be your item criticism channel, your client experience meeting, and even your initial admonition framework for when things went amiss.

Gamify: People appreciate rivalry and like being compensated for accomplishments, and including game-like components into your showcasing blend can assist you with inspiring a network. Foursquare is one successful case of this, moving its clients through mayorships and identifications. You can distinguish approaches to incent your locale in manners that line up with your business objectives, making a drawing in with your image fun. This can be an incredible method to build the number of answers your locale is giving in an assistance discussion—include levels and accomplishments for responding to questions, for top-notch responses, or for sharing out unanswered inquiries. Coordinate conduct and objectives with remuneration frameworks. Organizations like Badgeville and BigDoor have items that can assist you in utilizing virtual prizes. These endeavors can expand on your current social showcasing, expanding slant, maintenance, and dependability, all while diminishing agitate, securing cost, and client support costs.

Reliable marking and voice

Numerous components go into a brand—both visual and something else—in any case, what it becomes is your guarantee to your clients. You characterize their experience of what your item offering attempts to satisfy. A "brand" can feel like a vague idea, yet consider the way that your organization's image causes to increase the value of the association. When overseen fittingly, it can assist with securing the ventures made to the business after some time. How one decides the estimation of a brand is a genuinely confusing undertaking.

The vast majority of us aren't attempting to contend with the most critical worldwide brands. That being stated, there sure is a ton you can gain from them:

Test Guidelines

1.   How your logo is to be spoken to

2.   What textual styles and hues can be utilized and in what way

3.   A full brand portrayal and a big motivator for it

4.   Situations in which the brand can and can't be utilized

5.   Tone, voice, and way rules

6.   Other geological and auxiliary components (basically for sponsors)

If you don't know as of now have brand rules created, you'll need to begin there with your promoting group. When you have those completed, you'll need to deliver how they mean social media. The majority of the visual segments (logos, hues, and so on.) will continue as before. However, you'll need to ensure the clients set up your social profiles approach any related, innovative resources. For more motivation, investigate the Cambridge Identity Guidelines and MailChimp's rules. For generally little and medium organizations, these will probably feel overeager (they likely are), yet you can gather motivation for the parts that bode well for you. If you have a visual computerization group, they ought to have the option to assist you with a great deal of this too.

Know your crowd: Be on-brand, yet additionally be pertinent to the earth in which you're working. Your group, or the social stage you are connecting on, may marginally change your tone and voice from your image rules. This is the place it's imperative to have an extremely strong seeing so you can adjust as necessary. It's not essential to be steady between stages, yet it is vital to show cohesiveness.

Be human: It likely sounds self-evident. However, this is the objective of social media. Personal commitment is the place the enchantment is, and remember that as you're building up your image will assist you with creating a voice that is strong and durable, yet also one that clients can identify with and manufacture associations with. You know, similar to individuals. :)

Incorporate your battles: Incorporating your crusades over the entirety of your social profiles can help set your image and intensify your endeavors. Utilizing comparable visual components over the whole of your patterns will help imbue your informing and commute home the point in manners that are applicable and tweaked to the stage.

Your social nearness is only an expansion of your image, permitting that brand to contact a lot more individuals through arranged encounters. This can be both a hazard and a chance, so it's essential to invest the energy it takes to choose and characterize what your image will be in the social condition, as irregularity right now leads to a disconnected client experience (or even a negative effect). Essential inquiries to answer include:

What areour image voice and character?

What do we rely on, and what do we speak to?

What is our offer and separating factors?

What are our characterized visual marking components (logo, textual style, hues, and so forth.)?

If you don't respond to these inquiries first, your social nearness can veer toward one of two limits: Either your correspondence will appear to be reliable and corporate, and the individuals you're drawing in will feel like they're managing a robot, or your locale administrator will utilize their voice in your interchanges, prompting a conflicting or even inauthentic experience.

Giving a durable, marked client experience that is a skeptic of site, system, or the area will serve to arouse your locale's understanding of, the memory of, and ideally inclination for your image.

Step by step instructions to win nature, trust, and affability in your locale

Building notoriety around these three characteristics is a piece of what goes into building connections. We're all right now puddle attempting to achieve enormous things for our organizations, yet step back for a moment—we should alternately consider this. How would you fabricate connections disconnected or face to face? Building them online for your image isn't too unique.

Appear Basic: simply being available is the initial step. Be that as it may, it doesn't stop there. You need to keep appearing. Give individuals motivation to put resources into the relationship. If you don't demonstrate you're going to stay or fly in at any rate to some degree,usually, they don't have any motivation to associate with you in any case.

Be human. Be thoughtful. Be genuine. Be entertaining. Be conscious. Be sympathetic. Be everything you would anticipate that somebody should be toward you in each cooperation. Nobody can without much of a stretch identify with a dull character. If your exertion feels mechanized and relentless, you won't appear to be genuinely amiable. Additionally,excellent to recall: When you're connecting with somebody on social channels, it's ideal for accepting all cooperations are open.

Try not to be exclusionary: This makes an

equalization in your connections. You would prefer not to treat a chosen few so exceptionally that untouchables new to your image or record feel as though they're outwardly glancing in. Endeavor to make each individual you connect with and those watching, feel like they are extraordinary, and part of the group worth knowing.

Be off-subject: Firmly identified with being human, it is unquestionably alright to go off-theme once in a while. On the off chance that each tweet or Facebook post is just your showcasing, individuals will tire rapidly and leave. Turn it off on occasion. Post something important, yet maybe just extraneously. I appreciate a joke from time to time. Commend the special seasons or world occasions. Nobody likes to be showcased to continually, and that is not where the enchantment occurs!

Include esteem: Without a doubt, you can appear and make companions just by being amicable. However, you're a brand. You need more than only "companions." You're fabricating a system and attempting to set up your organization here. Including worth will assist you with being viewed as supportive and legitimate, and at last, make you a needed piece of the network. Offer help, answer questions and make a special effort to make somebody's life simpler or more splendid.

Practice manners. Try not to spam hashtags. Brands experience gotten in difficulty for this before, and it can show your image in an ill-bred and offensive light. Try not to be excessively pushy or advance; you need to establish a decent first connection.

Know about recent developments. During solemn occasions, catastrophic events, disasters, times of fear-based oppression, and so on., you certainly need to kill you're showcasing informing. In case you're utilizing a planning administration to post content for you, turn it off quickly whenever there's any hint of a cataclysmic occasion of any sort. Your planning will be viewed as amazingly coldhearted and could cause a severe reaction against your image.

None of this will occur for you medium-term. Interest in these connections is, at last, a long haul interest in your locale and brand. Keep it up, and show restraint—the more you contribute, the more you'll get back.

Emergency the board

We trust that we're never confronted with a

crisis as a business, and social media can include an additional layer of complexity to such a circumstance. An actual episode can be enhanced by informal organizations, throwing a shadow over all that you state, and client support issues can seethe and immediately spread through social stages. Simultaneously, however, interpersonal organizations can be an excellent method to rehearse straightforwardness, as the ideal approach to battle disarray is with clearness. Cushion, a social sharing application, exemplified this kind of reaction when it was hacked in late 2013. Their blog, and the remarks beneath it, are a demonstration of the advantages of open correspondence through social channels.

When pondering emergency the board, all organizations ought to be in one of the accompanying four phases consistently:

- Arrangement: Understanding dangers, working out heightening procedures, draft reactions, jobs, and duties, preparing, and so on.
- Reaction and estimation: Responding if fundamental, following up, estimating and checking reach, volume, and so forth.

- Recuperation: Typically comprises higher estimation, development, contextual investigations, and information sharing all through the association.
- Avoidance: Analysis of emergency and existing techniques, recognizable proof of chances for development, and affirmation of what functioned admirably.

When in emergency mode, work to initially comprehend the degree of seriousness, distinguish potential dangers, and raise likewise. Work through the emergency by listening eagerly, demonstrating sympathy, straightforwardness, and an eagerness to address whatever wrong had been finished. Sometime later, inspecting the effect and pulling understanding from the circumstance can enable the association to mend, push ahead, and gain footing toward a solid safeguard act.

FINDING THE RIGHT SOCIAL NETWORK

NETWORK
Choosing where to center your online life

vitality can be a befuddling procedure, as time is short and assets are restricted. It's anything but difficult to get diverted by the buzz and articles touting the following significant thing that brands "must do." As with any promoting channel, however, the more idea and methodology you put into your usage designs, the more prominent your possibility of achievement. You can abstain from being overpowered by venturing back and beginning with your business destinations, item contributions, and target buyers.

What are the various kinds of social channels?

Not every single social medium locales and stages are made equivalent, and every social channel won't generally work a similar route in helping clients arrive at their objectives. In looking over the online condition, it assists with arranging your social alternatives into classifications. By taking a gander at gatherings of channels with healthy subjects, it is simpler to outline your choices about when, where, who, and how best to connect with your locale on the web.

The most straightforward approach to separate the classifications is to consider them claimed, leased, and involved. Here arehow every one of those classifications separates:

Possessed properties

Possessed properties may incorporate web journals, gatherings, or homegrown informal organizations, and they can be inside or outside. The primary distinction with this classification is that you possess the channel as opposed to involving a page on a stage that is claimed by another person. It might be on your essential site or another space, yet it is entirely heavily influenced by you.

Leased properties

Much like leasing a condo, a client possesses a bit of a channel with the authorization of the proprietor. Here and there is a cost included, however in the realm of internet-based life, that doesn't occur frequently. Locales like Facebook, Twitter, and Tumblr fall into this class. Facebook possesses its site, and you're dealing with a nearness on it. You may have an official case to the page, yet you have no evidence to the stage itself or a state by the way it might change.

Involved properties

This classification is the most expelled from

your control. Your organization may have an official agent who cooperates and takes part in an associated feature. However, there is no responsibility for kind, and these channels can be changed whenever. Reddit is likely the most well-known model. Representatives of an organization will often take an interest in gatherings or network destinations in either an official or informal limit, yet consistently in the interest of the organization. Shopper discussions happen over every one of the three of these social channel classes; however, before you jump into any of them, it's critical to take some time and thoroughly consider your channel the executive's plans and interest procedures. For instance, littler brands with restricted assets may choose one site dependent on the high mileage they can get from their buyer base before expecting to fan out into various channels. As a delegate of your image, you have the chance to increase the value of whatever channel will work best for your association.

Which system would it be a good idea for me to pursue first?

There is nobody answer to this inquiry. For every single business, this inquiry will be addressed unexpectedly. A decent initial step for any association is to visit KnowEm.com. This site permits you to enlist your image name across more than 500 informal organizations. This will assist with guaranteeing that your name will be obtained where you need it to be, paying little heed to which stage you wind up choosing is directly for your image. Also, for those that you should not have to utilize immediately, your image name stays shielded from squatters. Like this, Knowem additionally has one of the most thorough arrangements of the entirety of the informal organizations on the web, so it is likewise a decent spot to search for systems past the undeniable Facebook, Twitter, Google+, and so forth.

It's a quite sure thing to state that almost everybody ought to have a Facebook page. With over 1.19 billion dynamic month to month clients (as of Sep. 2013), you will likely locate a substantial number of your clients here. You may find something very similar on Twitter. Another instrument to assist you with narrowing down the "where" of your common technique is to go on somewhat of a listening venture. Utilize one of the numerous social listening apparatuses to discover where your clients and more noteworthy industry are having applicable discussions. This knowledge should help reveal where it bodes well to set up your essence.

Single versus numerous records

Regardless of whether to endeavor multiplefiles on one informal organization is an unavoidable issue. The appropriate response: It depends. Some large organizations, as Nordstrom, have a corporate Twitter account, while a significant number of their stores have their records. This permits them to convey rather explicit and tremendous data to provincial supporters while keeping up their corporate record for general news, advancements, and declarations. Different organizations have thought that it was useful to section their careers by item, for example, Google, GoogleAPIs, Blogger, etc. Right now, bodes well dependent on their contributions to split the discussions by crowd and piece as opposed to topography. Nike, Comcast, and Delta Airlines are genuine instances of brands that have effectively actualized different records for various purposes. The most significant interesting point when choosing if it bodes well to fragment your profiles on these systems is whether you're better ready to increase the value of the client and the discussion. Is it true that you are better prepared to address your client's needs on one record, or are there territorial contemplations that may make that progressively troublesome?

Moreover, you ought to painstakingly think about your capacity to deal with various records. Instruments like Hootsuite, Sprout Social, and SocialEngage make it simpler than any time in recent memory to deal with different files from one dashboard. Yet, recall— there's nothing more troubled than a surrendered social record. It doesn't send a decent message about your image and its capacity to finish.

The most effective method to begin

First of all, ask yourself a couple of inquiries:

•   What conduct am I attempting to drive, and to what business end?

•   Of the social channels out there, which types loan themselves to the particular items or potential benefits I offer?

•   Who are my objective clients, and what do I think about their online conduct?

Distinguishing your objectives will assist you with choosing which sort of online life channel puts forth the most sense for your attempts, and explaining the ideal conduct of your locale individuals will help characterize how you approach drawing in with them. For instance, would you say you are attempting to expand brand mindfulness? Assuming this is the case, consider advertising exercises that incorporate the assortment and sharing of client tributes, profoundly shareable substance, and buzz-commendable connections. Is it accurate to say that you are going for expanded traffic and transformations? Search for chances to draw in with valuable, intrigued clients who are prepared to pull the "purchase" trigger. The fact is to coordinate your commitment endeavors with the results you need to see.

How about we take a gander at a model. Envision you're running a developing delight items organization with enormous national and worldwide goals. Here's a bit by bit guide to picking the correct social stage for that business:

Try not to restrain your intuition to vertical. Go level as well.

Indeed, your clients are keen on your items' specialty; however, shouldn't something be said about their different advantages and subjects—the ones by implication adjusted to your hobby? For instance, say you're a retailer of cruising vessels and rigging. There are, without a doubt, some stunning cruising related networks that bode well for you to approach. Yet, there's a high probability that your clients additionally have a substantial level of enthusiasm for movement, other outside exercises, and maybe even nourishment and wine. Consider how you might take an interest in those flat networks, and make proper acquaintance with a tremendously extended crowd!

Concentrate on what is generally critical to your locale as opposed to what is usually famous

When you get moving in social, it's anything but difficult to get diverted. There are new applications, apparatuses, and systems that spring up on a nearly everyday schedule, and you could without much of a stretch spend your whole day merely looking at them all. The thought, however, is to find some kind of harmony between devices fixated promoting and being an ostrich with its head in the sand. It's smarter to do fewer things successfully than numerous things incapably. Be that as it may, you ought likewise to keep your eyes and ears open for the exceptional social patterns; there will be the point at which it bodes well for you to hop in. Here are a few interesting points:

•	Look for stage functionalities that work with your item offering or market space. For instance, garments retailers are very much situated for the picture sharing informal communities that have gotten well known, like Instagram and Pinterest.

•	Emerging innovations and additionally usefulness that permit you to convey and impart to your locale in new manners.

•	Additionally, look out for advances and destinations that can arrive at new socioeconomics that fall inside your intended interest group or their influencers.

At the point when all else comes up short, watch out for your objectives, yet don't be reluctant to dunk your toes in the water and test, test, test. Contribute enough vitality so you can get a critical reaction and utilize this as your directing light on whether you ought to go further.

As new systems develop, how would you dispatch another nearness?

In internet based life, there are sure realities and standards. When you've applied those to your business in propelling a nearness on one system, you will rapidly observe that they are compact across about every single other system. The principles of commitment may vary marginally from site to site, as will the semantics, maybe, however, the basics will stay unaltered paying little heed to the stage and are consistently the best spot to begin when spreading out.

Objectives and estimation: Determining your new channel's objectives ought to be something you consider from the earliest starting point. For what reason would you say you are connecting on this new channel? What are you attempting to receive in return? After you have recognized your objectives, you need to conclude how to gauge your prosperity. For rising stages, this may take some time, contingent upon what examination instruments are accessible in the commercial center and how the stage's API is set up. (You could generally construct your own if it's sufficiently open and you have the assets.)

Marking: Your social authority is essential, and compelling naming can go far to set up your power as a brand. Social channels additionally furnish you with energizing prospects to communicate your image and increment brand impressions. Ensure your symbols are on point, and your profiles are dialed in, and make the most of your early introduction!

Content seeding: There is nothing very as dismal as visiting the page of a social profile you're keen on and finding nothing there. Before you begin following individuals or expertly guiding traffic to your new profile, ensure you post some substance through the span of a few days. This consoles guests that there is something there worth after.

Influencer association: After you get your marking t's crossed and your substance I'm specked, it's an ideal opportunity to begin searching for individuals with whom you can lock-in. Start by searching out those people you've recognized as influencers from different stages. You have likely previously settled a relationship with them, and connections are compact across steps. Influence that. As you connect with them, search out more people who are pertinent to your space in their devotees. After a short time, you ought to have the reason for a decent system.

Revelation: Once you have built up this new system is where you plan on contributing time and vitality, add joins from famous spots to enable your clients to find your new nearness. Review content about what you're doing that is fascinating, and feature it on your blog. Cross-post from your other social channels to drive mindfulness.

Content schedule/distributing: As with the entirety of different channels you have set up, it's imperative to keep a substance or to spreadthe agenda. You can make some substance booking through accessible instruments like HootSuite, Sprout Social, and SocialEngage. When arranging a substance schedule, you can be as advanced as having a module heated directly into your substance the board framework or as basic as utilizing an Excel spreadsheet. It's hugely about whatever works for you, and preparing assists with guaranteeing you're ultimately enhancing occasions, advancements, and interests pertinent to your crowd.

At the point when you're prepared to begin, there can be such a significant amount to do that it appears to be overpowering. The extraordinary thing about social, however, is that once you get the rudiments settled, a large portion of them are transferable to whatever new site tags along that you need to attempt. These accepted procedures will assist you in setting yourself up for achievement in social paying little heed to your size or what the stage is.

HOW TO BUILD A WONDERFUL PROFILE
Component #1: Your profile name

OK, this appears to be genuinely fundamental. The name that shows on your social media profile should simply be your name, isn't that so? Ordinarily, that is right. In any case, some of the time, that doesn't bode well.

On stages like Twitter, where you don't need to utilize theright name, an alias bode well. For instance, James Chartrand isn't the good name of the lady behind Men With Pens. However, that is the name on her Twitter account since that is how she's known in the business.

Component #2: Your username and URL

On most informal organizations, your username is remembered for your URL, and it's frequently unique about your showcase name. For the most part, you can't change your username, so pick it cautiously. On the off chance that conceivable, it's usually best to simply go with your name. Be that as it may, some of the time, in case you're the substance of your organization, the organization name may work better.

On Twitter, Brian Dean isn't @briandean; however, @backlinko, since that is the name of his organization. At long last, while it isn't always conceivable, attempt to keep your username the equivalent across stages. It very well may be confounding when this isn't the situation, as Instagram being @yourname and Twitter being @yourcompany or @yourmiddlename.

Component #3: Your profile pic

Would it be a good idea for you to go with a logo or an individual picture? If it's for a personal record, you ought to quite often go with a headshot. In any case, shouldn't something be said about for an organization? It's an intense call, yet it indeed relies upon your objectives. On the off chance that you run a little activity, or are the substance of your organization, incorporate a headshot of you. That is the thing that James and Brian do on Twitter, even with organization usernames. This additionally applies to individuals that are brands themselves, similar to artists, specialists, or government officials. Yet, on the off chance that you have an increasingly conspicuous brand or don't need your organization to be related with you explicitly, go with the logo.

It's additionally a smart thought to stay with the equivalent (or possibly a comparative) photograph across various informal communities. That way, you're simpler to perceive in multiple stages.

Component #4: Your connection

This differs starting with one social media arrange then onto the next, yet make sure to search out any chance to get your link on the principle page of your social profile. For instance, you can include a connection to the "first-page" of your profiles on Twitter and LinkedIn. Ensure that your relationship is upfront with the goal that individuals can discover it rapidly and navigate to your site. Another smart thought for your connections is to make an informal organization-specific point of arrival so you can follow which profiles are bringing your website the most traffic.

You can utilize these pages to offer a unique markdown for individuals who have discovered you on Twitter or offer data that is explicit to a system, similar to ongoing blog entries you have expounded on Facebook.

Component #5: Your profile

Your original social profile bio usually is only a sentence or two about yourself or your business. Consider it an ideal spot to put your lift pitch and incorporate watchwords. In a couple of words, what might you say about your business? It's likewise a smart thought to utilize your profile to its fullest potential. A few locales, similar to Twitter, just let you compose a short depiction. Be that as it may, in case you're on a stage like LinkedIn, your "outline" can have up to 2,000 characters. This is a tremendous chance to clarify what you're about and establish an extraordinary first connection.

To cause this to succeed, you'll need to include something beyond an essential depiction of what you've done and your present activities. Instead, make a story with a critical source of inspiration. For instance, you can tell how you began with the business you're working in. What got you keen on it, and what makes you stay and continue learning? At long last, you can complete your profile with a straightforward source of inspiration. This can be a connection to a free report, an idea for somebody to call you, or even a statement of purpose asking, "will you go along with me?"

Component #6: Your inclinations

A few profiles permit you to have extra expanded data about yourself as most loved books, network shows, motion pictures, etc. Many individuals skirt this, particularly with regards to business profiles. However, that is a severe mix-up. Take a gander at these fields as an extra spot to get some incredible worth and associations

I question there is a specialty out there that doesn't have in any event a couple of distributed books. Discover books, narratives, and profiles of influential individuals in your industry and include those in these extra fields (accepting you appreciate them, obviously!). This provides believability and another degree of association you can work with individuals who are finding out about you just because.

Component #7: Your experience or spread picture

Various states have various prerequisites. However, most informal communities today have some approach to include a bigger picture behind your primary profile page. A few clients, particularly on Twitter and LinkedIn, decide to utilize the default foundation picture, yet this is a slip-up. A modified foundation will permit you to share extra data and offer character to you or your image.

Try not to make it diverting or more significant than your profile picture, yet an extraordinary spread picture can go far to customizing your social page. On certain stages, like Facebook, this can even be a video. On the off chance that you have the alternative (and not too bad video), this can also be a considerably all the more captivating approach to associate with others.

Component #8: Your security settings

So after you have the entirety of your profile rounded out and pictures transferred, the following thing that you should investigate your security settings. These shifts from system to organize, yet you will need to ensure that the data you might want to be open is visible. Odds are, if this is a business-related profile, you'll need almost everything to be free. If your profile is of a progressively close to home nature, you might need to shroud a few things.

Component #9: Your movement

When your profile arrangement is finished, your progressing crucial be to keep up a substantial degree of action on your informal principle organizations. It's insufficient to leave a profile clear! You have to add to the stage and construct associations. That is what they're there for in any case. Regardless of what informal organization you're on, the fundamental rules despite everything apply. You'll need to interface with companions and devotees by posing inquiries and reacting to remarks.

Offer some incentive by posting fascinating thoughts, or possibly sharing intriguing and significant things you find. Furthermore, in case you're in any gatherings, become a functioning member—be useful, associate with others in the group, and offer things the audience will discover intriguing.

Component #10: Your advancement

At last, there is not at all like a little wellbeing advancement of your interpersonal organization profiles to assist more with peopling discover and interface with you. Make sure to include your interpersonal interaction profile connects to your site, email mark, and business card. Likewise, remember to interlink your profiles to one another. Numerous systems have spots to incorporate links to different systems, and you can and should utilize them at whatever point conceivable. Remain associated, become a functioning part of your preferred interpersonal organization, and you'll begin obtaining an after.

End

In case you're beginning with social media advertising, the initial step is to set up your records and profiles accurately. On the off chance that you've just been in the game for some time, it's likely time to investigate the patterns you set up. Are there approaches to improve what you as of now have on the web? Is the profile picture you transferred a year ago still significant? Does your profile or connection need refreshing? Since it'll be the early introduction numerous individuals see, it merits investing some energy to improve your social media nearness and make it convincing and fascinating.

HOW TO GROW YOUR PERSONAL OR BUSINESS BRAND ON SOCIAL MEDIA

In case you're a brand today, there's a non-zero possibility you're via web-based networking media somehow or another, shape, or structure. Be that as it may, what number of brands have a functioning, flourishing internet based life nearness? What's more, what amount of them are simply kind of there? Rude awakening: you can't expect much from social when you post irregular connections, @mention a couple of people, and consider it daily. You need some structure. You need an online life procedure

To build up an unshakable individual brand, you have to set up yourself as a dependable, legitimate voice in your industry. Subsequently, you could create extra customers or grab the attention of a potential boss, which could assist you in taking your vocation or business to the following level.

While building your image online can be anything besides the simple, different informal communities can improve the procedure. Discover how to develop your vision via web-based networking media.

Refine Your Social Presence

It is essential just to have one social profile for every stage on the web, and you should erase other records that could confound your objective segment. Also, you should audit your profile and expel any questionable posts that could detrimentally affect your image.

Cautiously Write a Social Media Description

Most remarkable online life channels will furnish their clients with a chance to compose a short depiction of themselves or a business. To build your quality, you should write a rundown of your aptitudes and interests in the representation. It won't just educate a potential adherent about what your identity is and what you do. However, they will fill in as amazing catchphrases, which can assist your image with appearing in the properly indexed lists and can make it simple for others to discover you on the web.

Launch an Attractive Website

If you need to turn into an idea chief in a particular industry, you should endeavor to turn into a reliable asset. Consequently, you should dispatch an alluring, straightforward to utilize the site to advance your image. You would then be able to distribute content onto your website and, like this, onto your social stages to produce traffic and increment your image mindfulness. In any case, don't adhere to an exhausting format that neglects to supplement your picture and put resources into a website specialist's information and skill. Assuming, in any case, you don't have the accounts accessible to subsidize a groundbreaking website architecture or the capacity to make sure about an advance from a bank, discover increasingly about terrible credit advances.

Crosslink to Your Other Social Media Accounts

When your site is ready for action, and you

have propelled different online networking efforts, you should enhance your records. For instance, you can build your web-based after crosslinking to your various profiles. For example, you can mean three web addresses onto your LinkedIn profile with the goal that you can guide your adherents to your site and two of your most fantastic internet based life pages.

Draw in with Your Audience

To develop your own image's mindfulness and structure robust associations with individuals over your industry, you should routinely draw in with your intended interest group on the web. For instance, you could compose a remark on somebody's tweet, or you could get engaged with various discussions or gatherings. LinkedIn and Facebook, as of now, offer a vast number of groups you can join at your recreation, so you can enter conversations on various themes and could even begin your own. It is an extraordinary method to associate with individuals from varying backgrounds, which can prompt a more grounded following and a higher system.

Maintain a strategic distance from Over-posting

Numerous individuals accept the way into a reliable online life following is to post content onto their channels usually. While you shouldn't leave your record dormant for significant periods, you should abstain from distributing various self-serving posts onto your Facebook, Twitter, and Instagram pages, which might exhaust your intended interest group. Instead, plan to post close to four to five self-serving advertisements every week, which ought to be blended with fun substance, for example,

Outsider substance

Crowd questions

Eye-catching challenges

Keep up a Consistent Image and Tone of Voice

Each expert needing to build up a reliable individual brand must make a predictable brand character. You won't possibly adhere to similar standards and convictions when posting via web-based networking media. However, you likewise should keep up the same manner of speaking and picture style, which can maintain a strategic distance from disarray when contacting your crowd.

Examine the Best Industry Influencers

On the off chance that you need to turn into a reliable voice of your industry and significantly develop your following, guarantee you cautiously break down different mainstream influencers from your industry. It will assist you in identifying their viable posting propensities, incredible substance procedures, and how they routinely interface with their devotees. On the off chance that you can distinguish their marking methodologies, you could before long apply the strategies into your own to build up an incredible battle that causes you to hang out in your industry.

FACEBOOK, TWITTER, YOUTUBE AND PINTEREST

FACEBOOK

When Facebook began in 2004, it was a stripped-down informal community concentrated on associating understudies. Nine years and more than 1 billion dynamic clients later, Facebook has become the most broadly utilized friendly community to date and has molded online association as we probably are aware of it. From interfacing far off loved ones to conquering any hindrance among brands and their networks, Facebook has taken how we connect online to an unheard-of level.

How are individuals utilizing Facebook?

Since its beginning, Facebook has become a necessary part of individuals' online social nearness. For some, Facebook is the leading online interpersonal organization in which they take an interest. However, the degree of commitment differs over the client range. From those that check the system occasionally during the time to the habitually dynamic individuals, the center's main impetus to investment is an association: interfacing with partners, companions old and new, graduated class systems, and for an expanding level of clients, even proficient associations.

The system itself has changed into one with profoundly adaptable protection and perceivability settings. Clients can dial down their permeability to where they are almost undetectable on the stage. They can pick which posts or updates are unmistakable and to whom. On the other hand, those clients who have chosen an all the more in with no reservations approach can leave everything open, from the pictures they're labeled into their dynamic stream on Spotify.

Highlights go past the individual client's page to mark pages, occasions, gatherings, and now a pseudo-independent emissary administration. The audience are client made and have fluctuating degrees of protection and security, much like individual profiles. Clients can arrange bunches around any subject or occasion they like. From expertly applicable gatherings to those sorted out around unique interests, for example, sustenance, the assortment is constrained distinctly by the enthusiasm of the clients. These gatherings have, without a doubt, been a greeting and clingy expansion to the stage after some time.

Occasions permit clients to sort out around a point in time. Security here is genuinely adaptable, taking into consideration open, private, and someplace in the middle of occasions. A key component here is the prepared incapacity to send out your Facebook occasions to different schedules, almost certainly expanding use and dependence on this element that mixes clients' close to home and expert lives.

Business pages have been a transformative item for Facebook. Throughout the years, they have taken a few distinct shapes. However, they are genuinely steady today. Like different sorts of pages, the list of capabilities is ever-advancing as they add more to address the issues of the advertisers behind the brand's endeavors. Facebook has, as of late, including more highlights regarding the investigation, detailing, security, and access, just as expanded the extravagance accessible to those wishing to plunge into Facebook promoting.

Facebook Messenger is another approach to consolidate email, moment ambassador, and Facebook messages. As a new independent gathering message administration sprung up all through 2010 and 2011, Facebook observed a chance and procured one of the more public gathering informing applications known as Beluga. They have since re-marked this application like Facebook Messenger. On iOS, Blackberry, and Android gadgets, this is an independent application, yet it likewise incorporates over the Facebook application and web encounters.

As clients progressively depend on social stages, these interpersonal organizations will develop and react as Facebook has. While there's still a lot of chance right now, it offers clients the most decision for the numerous features of their lives while empowering adaptability for protection and permeability. As clients keep on receiving new practices and at last desires, Facebook should keep on adjusting to remain at the highest point of the social heap, so anticipate proceeded with change and advancement. This change is fundamental and gainful; however,it can be disappointing from an advertising point of view.

Techniques and strategies for progress

As an ever-increasing number of individuals and brands hop onto Facebook, the commotion level for singular clients increments. While Facebook's News Feed calculation enables the clamor to level by indicating clients what it esteems the most significant substance, to stand apart from the group indeed, brands must be excellent, fascinating, and include esteem. To guarantee your content is seen, you'll have to enhance and consider Facebook-explicit usefulness.

Content: Everything you post on Facebook is content. As we presently know from the News Feed calculation, how clients collaborate with that substance is significant. Consider each bit of material you post an open door for expanded and explicit commitment and don't be reluctant to have a ton of fun. Investigate these models from Delta and GE. While on-brand, you can see they're somewhat startling and show they're not hesitant to show their human side. By and large, 39% greater commitment.

Post timing: Also identified with the elements

of your substance is when and how you post it. Be sure you're following what time of day your fans are generally dynamic. Centering your commitment during these occasions will assist you with developing your locale. Likewise, make sure to focus on things like sentence structure, expressing, and kinds of posts that are especially captivating to your crowd. Numerous Facebook clients check the site on their mid-day breaks, and after supper and keeping in mind that the last is outside of ordinary business hours, it merits testing to check whether that is the point at which your crowd is searching for content.

Control: Brands have expanding levels of duty regarding client created content posted on their dividers or in remarks. You'll need to proactively consider your position on the improper substance on your Facebook page, and your best practice is to make this position openly accessible. This tells your locale what you will and won't permit, reduces the opportunity of amazement, and constructs a feeling of wellbeing and sets desires.

Facebook is an open and open space, so you can't control everything individuals state. Examples in which it is suitable to evacuate client substance would include advertorial substance, provocation and misuse, slanderous or hostile language, compromising posts, and posts that contain touchy data (Visa numbers, addresses, and so forth.). Examples in which you should address the remarks as opposed to evacuating them include client protests, negative discourse, and necessary explanations. You dislike what individuals consistently need to state, however in social;you generally need to tune in.

Commitment: Because we are building something established, seeing someone, you can exploit by participating in discussions with your clients. They need to interface with your image and are making a special effort to do as such. Respect that. The sort of debate will direct the rhythm and musicality of your reaction. This is, to a great extent, reliant on your item too; for instance, a carrier's reaction rates to client support issues should be reasonably fast, as their clients' needs are likely definitely additional time-delicate than those in another industry. No one, but you can figure out what is directly for your association and item. Yet, at any rate in the underlying phases of building a network, it's smarter to decide in favor of quicker reactions.

Network: Make your crowd's understanding on

Facebook about their experience and their associations as opposed to your CTR and change rates. Focus on them, and you'll succeed. Your crowd will transform into a network that flourishes, develops, and underpins each other. By empowering commitment inside the group, you can help increment the degree of tenacity and partiality they should the brand, advancing toward client support.

Client stream: While the page condition Facebook gives brands is for the most part set, you need to ensure you're coordinating your clients where you need them to go. On the off chance that I am a client searching for help or help, will I realize where to go? Similarly, as you do, when planning greeting pages for your site, consider the objectives of your Facebook page. What do you need clients to do when they land on your page? What data do they should have the option to get to no problem at all? Ensure these components are upfront. You can, without much of a stretch, change the request for the applications and even enhance the symbols used to show those applications for permeability. JetBlue is an incredible case of a consistent and clear client stream.

Validity: A large piece of your image is based

on trust, and the establishment of that trust is your believability. Syntax and spelling are all-around significant, and all endeavors for their right uses ought to be made. Actuality check sources and news before sharing them on your systems. Guarantee the wellbeing of your clients by not sharing connects to malevolent locales. Ensure you don't give your locale motivation to trust you are something besides what you are: great.

Etiquette tips and rules

Like disconnected social cooperations, Facebook has its arrangement of unwritten dos and don'ts for clients to follow. Facebook is, above all else, an interpersonal organization that worked to assist clients with remaining associated with each other. It has additionally advanced into a stage for organizations to draw in with their clients. This chain of command is critical to remember and implies that you should realize the ropes before making a plunge. Here are a couple of tips to kick you off with legitimate Facebook behavior:

Try not to spam: This is a significant no through the entirety of promoting. Continuously be prudent, tasteful, and don't spam. This incorporates sending mass-occasion welcomes and messages and solicitations to like your image pages from your record. It's not challenging to spam as a business page, either. However, Facebook's usefulness forestalls its majority.

React: Response times will differ depending on the issue and the item being referred to, yet in social media, practicality is essential. Clients anticipate that things should happen a lot quicker on social channels than on increasingly customary web channels like email. Much of the time, same-day reactions are required. Never let your locale feel like they've been overlooked.

Disapprove of bunched refreshes: With the particular case of picture collections, abstain from making different updates inside a brief timeframe length. Past News Feed algorithmic concerns, it's merely irritating to your supporters. Your sign to-commotion proportion falls, and you may lose the long haul consideration of your crowd.

@Name: If you need to get out another open Facebook page or client, you can get legitimately connection to their Facebook page, which likewise tells them that you're discussing them by putting a @ and afterward composing

their name. (Facebook will assist your determination with a drop-down.) This likewise makes it more clear to whom you're tending to. Note that private clients can't be called out right now you're answering to a remark they left on your page.

Feature significant posts: If your image has any substantial updates, for example, acquisitions, deals, or highlight in news stories, you can feature them in your page's timetable. This extends the post to the two segments and may get these significant updates further into individuals' News Feeds.

Messages: People can send your page private messages. You'll locate the majority of these messages will be client assistance related, so make a point to check them—the messages segment capacities like an email inbox.

Warnings: The notices box will show you the latest preferences, remarks, divider posts, and so forth., on your image's page. Contingent upon the volume of approaching movement, this regulatory area can be valuable when following action by your locale. Because of Facebook's emphasis on slowchange, you'll presumably just get remarks and likes on late posts. However, the warnings can help track action on more established posts.

Page top picks: You can stamp other brand pages as top choices on your business' page. This is a useful method to advance accomplices, great motivations, or others you're interfacing your business with.

Posting: While numerous social media devices permit you to present from them on Facebook, you'll have the best outcomes by submitting legitimately on Facebook from Facebook itself. Facebook's calculation predispositions toward posts that start from its interface. Reactions and remark control, in any case, should be possible using social administration programming without issue.

Planning: Thankfully, Facebook allows booking of posts straightforwardly in their interface. If you are sharing connected substance, this substance should, as of now, be live on the web, which can be a pickle for those planning unpublished blog entries or other materials. Booked presents will show up just on the arbitrators in the "Action Log." Keep as a main priority. However, that commitment is an essential objective, and you'll need to be around for the reactions to your planned posts.

TWITTER

Beginning On Twitter

Twitter can be gotten to through a PC, yet also through your web empowered telephone. You can send a solitary message to one or various clients, fellow companions, and read messages sent to you absent a lot of trouble. Be that as it may, on the off chance that you are entirely new to this person to person communication administration, here is a simple manual to assist you with beginning and moving.

Twitter messages, generally known as tweets, are comprised of up to 140 characters, much like an SMS. You can, in any case, say much in such not many words, cant you? This is an angle that makes Twitter experience enchanting. You can create an impression on a gathering of clients or a solitary client, or discuss straightforwardly with companions you have followed (and have tailed you) with short tweets like "I'll be going to the late spring gig this end of the week, you may join." This tells what your arrangements are and on the off chance that they mean to go along with you.

In twitter, there is extraordinary adaptability

with regards to picking what to make open and what not to. You can create an impression on a specific companion without others seeing the message, and you can also impart some data to an area of companions. Your general profile can likewise be made private or open. If you don't want your twitter ID to be accessible to anybody, at that point, you can set so.

On the off chance that you don't have a twitter account, joining is very basic, and it's free. Simply go to www.twitter.com and top in the close down structure with your name email and secret word. It is prescribed to utilize your right name with the goal that companions will effortlessly remember you. Else you may have nobody tailing you since you have used an exciting title that they are inexperienced with. It is likewise critical to transfer a profile picture so those companions who don't recall you by name can perceive your photograph.

When you have your twitter account set, now is the ideal time currently to get companions to tail you. You can send then your twitter address, which is regularly as twitter.com/yourusername. For instance, on the off chance that your username is Ryman, at that point, your twitter page address will be twitter.com/ryman. You can also discover individuals you know on twitter. Visit their pages and snap "follow." Building a system of numerous companions in twitter makes the entire experience increasingly fun and advantageous

Buying into On Twitter's Bandwagon

On the off chance that you don't have a Twitter account yet, you more likely than not been thinking about what is so beguiling about it that every one of your people is in that wagon. Twitter is a long-range interpersonal communication site that empowers individuals to share thoughts through short messages famously known as tweets. Twitter is considered as a miniaturized scale blogging administration because of the clients' capacity to post data as writings, pictures, and recordings and offer with companions over the globe.

Pursuing a Twitter account

Getting a record in Twitter is essential; all you need is to go to the site, hit the sign up the catch, and give your fundamental data like username, secret key, and your email. At that point, you can set your profile with your extra insights about yourself, for example, marital status, your area, and a concise depiction of what your identity is and what you like. You can, too, transfer your photograph as a profile picture with the goal that your companions will remember you much, no problem at all. Inside a couple of moments of the setup, which is very basic, your Twitter record ought to be ready for action.

Getting companions to tail you

To have a superior tweeting involvement with Twitter, you have to get the same number of individuals tailing you. Following a companion implies you can share data either through tweeting or text talk. Even though your general profile might be open freely, just those companions whom you follow each other can impart data to you. You can pick what to partake in broad daylight and what not to. You can also choose the companions you need to follow and impart data to.

Why you ought to be on Twitter

One reason why you ought to have a Twitter account is that it turns out to be very simple to stay in contact with companions, make new companions and keep refreshed on what's going on around you. If you have a business, you can utilize Twitter to impart to your customers and let them know the sorts of items you are offering and at white costs.

Numerous organizations in your territory ought to likewise be having Twitter accounts. This implies you can find a workable pace they are selling and at which terms. This can help you in settling on spending decisions and guaranteeing you get the best arrangements without soliciting face to face fro from the organizations. There are unlimited advantages of being on Twitter, and the most helpful approach to realize these advantages is by pursuing a record.

YOUTUBE

After its modest beginnings in 2005, YouTube has gotten something beyond a spot to watch feline recordings. After eight years, YouTube has transformed into the world's second-biggest web index, a driver of online culture, and a springboard for Internet acclaim. There's still a lot of feline recordings to go around. However, YouTube has its sights on higher, better thoughts.

Key details and socioeconomics

- YouTube sees more than one billion exceptional visits every month

- Over 6 billion hours of video are observed every month

- 100 long stretches of video are transferred each moment

- Mobile gadgets represent more than 1 billion perspectives every day

- According to Nielsen, YouTube arrives at more US grown-ups ages 18-34 than any link arrange

- Thousands of YouTube channels are making six figures every year

How the system is being utilized by shoppers

In a word, sharing. Content is being transferred and shared through YouTube at record rates. Clients can follow channels (which have gotten progressively refined in their plan and usefulness throughout the years), move their substance, remark on and talk about recordings, and follow other clients' content. With the capacity to connect legitimately to or implant recordings, YouTube has become an essential wellspring of video diversion for clients everywhere throughout the web. Its ability to adapt through promotions—both for itself and its clients—includes a layer of monetary manageability.

Methodologies and strategies for progress

Commitment: The remarks on YouTube are famous for being somewhat of a no man's land. A considerable lot of them are trivial and regularly from trolls. Numerous brands shut off their remarks in light of current circumstances. You may pick to leave comments on, just to perceive what sort of commitment you get, and that is alright as well. What isn't prescribed, however, is to leave them on and overlook them; either keep an eye on the garden or dispose of it by and large. What's more, you can see amazing outcomes by deciding to connect with your crowd.

To improve remarking on YouTube, YouTube remarks are currently straightforwardly attached to G+ accounts. As a business, you'll have to interface your G+ image page and your image's YouTube account. To start with, you have to make your YouTube account a manager on your G+ page. At that point, ensure you're signed into your YouTube record and afterward adhere to YouTube's associate guidelines. In the wake of everything's associated, alarms for new remarks on your YouTube recordings will show up in your G+ warnings, and your YouTube recordings will appear in a tab on your G+ image page

Content Strategy:

Help content and other how-tos: For certain items, instructional exercises and how-tos will be inconceivably valuable. Help your crowd figure out how to all the more likely utilize your item, remembering thoughts regarding how to use your question for novel ways. Assist them with figuring out how to do things that may not be straightforwardly identified with your item, yet are exceptionally pertinent to their inclinations.

For instance, a clean nail brand may periodically feature how-tos for unique occasion hair. This is amazingly significant to their crowd, yet not straightforwardly identified with their item. This is a strategy we've referenced previously: think on a level plane.

Select substance: This can appear as early access to new items, unique channel-explicit special arrangements, or even insider organization news. Giving these constrained crowds elite access to various kinds of substances will cause them to feel regarded and "up to date." Also, making channel-explicit substance will give every individual motivation to tail you on more than one channel, expanding the profundity of their relationship.

Boost interest: Have your locale make substance and offer it for your sake over their systems. You, at that point, can clergyman dependent on hashtag or a focal archive (for example, a blog entry holding YouTube substance), or locate some other method to help cause to notice and interface the client stories. This action can drive consciousness of your essence and help connect with the crowd while eliminating the measure of work expected of you.

Estimation: Just like your other showcasing endeavors, you must recognize what achievement resembles. Tailor your efforts (content, commitment, and so on.) toward activities that assist you with moving the needle and demonstrate your prosperity by estimating progress against your recognized objectives.

Etiquette tips and rules

Connect dependably: If you have remarks

empowered on your recordings, ensure you moderate them and remain drew in, as YouTube is more inclined than different stages to create nasty comments. You'll need to provide your channel keeps on offering some incentive. If you happen to end up within sight of trolls (and the sun isn't out to go them to stone), make sure to keep your fresh; you follow up for the benefit of your image in an open discussion.

Remark carefully: Whether you have remarks empowered on your recordings or not, there are likely going to be times when you'll need (or need) to remark on different strings and recordings. The standard appeal applies there, also: don't shout at individuals, check your spelling and punctuation, utilize your image voice, and unquestionably don't leave malicious remarks yourself.

Promote securely: This isn't a choice to mess with. For high volume channels, it very well may be income delivery. However, that should be weighed against the brand sway and the clients' involvement in your substance.

Favoriting and buying in If you most loved a video, it likewise appears on your profile page as a video you favorited, offering it to your companions and endorsers. Buying into somebody's channel implies that you'll see the entirety of their most recent transfers and top picks in the feed on your page—this what might be compared to tailing somebody on Twitter.

Transferring recordings: Luckily, YouTube takes about each video group under the sun. Moving the video is the simple part, rounding out the data about the video is the genuine work. You need to ensure that your portrayal is SEO-and individuals improved, that your title and watchwords are on track, that your recordings are appropriately classified, and (if conceivable) that you give a transcript of every video. All of the applicable data you can add to your YouTube transfer gives you a higher open door for individuals to discover your video and makes it available for a wide range of clients and search bots.

PINTEREST

Through excellent pictures and simple to-utilize "sticking," this site has overwhelmed the online network. Following its beta dispatch in 2010, Pinterest gave an approach to clients to just share and make picture assortments for leisure activities, style, organizations, and the sky is the limit from there. Regardless of whether you're an entrepreneur interfacing with your clients through pictures or attempting to rearrange your home in DIY-design, Pinterest has something for pretty much everybody.

Key details and socioeconomics

• Pinterest has 20 million month to month dynamic clients (70 million enlisted clients)

• More than 50 million one of a kind guests for every month

• 5 million "article pins" every day

• Women are multiple times as likely as men to utilize Pinterest

• Pinterest clients in the US go through about an hour on the site every month

• Shoppers spend more on their buys when alluded from Pinterest—generally twice as much as referrals from Facebook and Twitter.

• Pinterest drives more referral traffic than Twitter, LinkedIn, and Reddit consolidated.

How are individuals utilizing Pinterest?

Picture based sharing is getting progressively significant for brands and purchasers the same. The viability of symbolism has driven destinations like Pinterest and Instagram to immediately turn into the new staples in day by day advanced life. In our current reality, where individuals would prefer fundamentally not to invest a ton of energy perusing, rich media enables clients to share, impart, and devour stories rapidly and effectively is essential manners.

Systems and strategies for progress

Commitment: The Pinterest people group is developing rapidly and can be locked in. This is an extraordinary open door for your customers to connect with you, so make sure to focus on your remarks for chances to have discussions. They might be posing inquiries or only offering expressions of acclaim or concern. Utilizing an instrument like PinAlerts or Pinterest's examination to screen where and how your substance is shared can assist you with getting open doors that don't come legitimately to you.

Content Strategy:

Feature clients: Highlight clients utilizing your item, the content they've made, or even their accounts. It will speak to their common want to be recognized and included. This additionally encourages them to feel like they've added an incentive back to their locale and imparts a feeling of proprietorship.

In the background: Give your crowd a look behind the drapery by displaying in the background pictures. This builds the sentiment of getting the uncommon restricted substance, and consequently, their partiality for your image.

Network relations: If your business is engaged with the network or functional cause exercises, share that with your crowd. You may feel like this puts on a show of being boasting. However, it tends to be done modestly and sacrificially. Your clients tail you since they've put resources into you and what you're doing, and your endeavors outside the workplace are an expansion of that relationship. You may even get them included!

Know your crowd: Know all that you can about your group and give them what they need to see. Diversion works exceptionally well on record, for instance, and lovely symbolism of any sort will work in general work extraordinarily well on Pinterest. You may even attempt to find a workable pace by investing energy in the stage in your profiles. You can utilize that to find a good pace works there and how individuals share and impart.

Discoverability: Set your site up to be shared socially on Pinterest. Ensure the social sharing catches on your substance pages are anything but difficult to discover and utilize. Guiding individuals' focus toward your Pinterest page will likewise assist them with finding your substance and empower partaking in new manners. Also,don't neglect to execute the proper following, so you know how well these are functioning!

Etiquette tips and rules

Give credit: Sharing others' substance is at the core of Pinterest, so giving appropriate credit is critical. In a perfect world, everything is stuck from its unique source, regardless of whether that implies burrowing a piece to discover it. You need to give the ideal client experience, and if you pin content legitimately from a Google Image SERP, for instance, clients would be connected back to that SERP rather than the page where the picture began.

*Change inscriptions:*Repinning isn't caring for retweeting on Twitter. You'll need to make sure to refresh the subtitle on a repinned pin to make it your own. It ought to speak to you and your image, and should demonstrate significance to your locale. Remember to utilize target catchphrases that your crowd looks for so they can without much of a stretch discover your pins.

Try not to flood: Pinning for the day will be a brand's most reliable option, and there are apparatuses to assist you with booking pins ahead of time. On the off chance that you pin the entirety of your substance without a moment's delay, you'll flood your adherents' streams, and it could bother them enough to unfollow your image.

Compose: Keep your sheets sorted out, as individuals will tail them for explicit substance. A client who buys into a "plans" board wouldn't like to see pictures of extravagant autos or fascinating furnishings. On the off chance that you need to share new kinds of substances, make new sheets.

Gathering sheets: Group sheets permit more than one client to stick to the board. You can team up with accomplice organizations, your colleagues, and any other person with whom you'd prefer to work together on one of a kind and fascinating substance. You'll undoubtedly need to have a technique and reason behind a mutual board.

Mystery sheets: This is likely not a component you'll use for your image. However, you can make sheets that are imparted to a constrained gathering of individuals and welcome them to nail to them also.

Confirm your site: In request to have a checked record and have Pinterest Analytics for your website, you'll have to confirm your website. Pinterest's Analytics will give you insights on what number of pins have been stuck from your site, what kind of traffic Pinterest drives to your site, and then some.

HOW TO MONETIZE YOUR SOCIAL MEDIA PAGE
GENERAL APPROACHES TO MONETIZE

Bringing in cash off web-based life isn't only for VIPs. With some cautious substance arranging and a reliable procedure, you can adapt your internet based life records and begin procuring pay directly from your telephone. You needn't bother with a considerable number of devotees to get paid to utilize web-based life; there are a lot of ways you can bring in cash online by adapting your records for nothing. Here are five of the ideal approaches to begin changing your online life profiles and gaining additional salary just by posting!

MAKE AN ONLINE COURSE

Know an ability that could profit others? Start an online class and sell your course for a low rate. The e-learning industry is quickly developing; these days, anybody with webcam and web association can show others and gain cash just by sharing their insight on the web. Your internet based life records will be critical to promoting your course, which you can have on locales like Kajabi and Udemy.

INCLUDE VIDEO MARKETING

Recordings increment client commitment ten times via web-based networking media; today, any robust substance procedure ought to incorporate video content over the web. It's evaluated that 80 percent of all web traffic will be video by 2019. Fusing video content into your social advertising system will, without a doubt, increment commitment and navigate rates and empower more noteworthy discussion.

BEGIN USING AD REVENUE PROGRAMS

Advertisements are perhaps the most reliable ways regular web clients started to bring in cash off their web-based social networking accounts. On the off chance that you have a blog or run a site, pursuing a program like Google Adsense will assist you with winning additional salary just by letting a few promotions run on your website. The way to being active with advertisement income via web-based networking media is to focus on your substance, as indicated by the sort of promotions that appeared on your page. You can offer an incentive through your posts that will urge guests to navigate and make a buy, which procures your salary.

USE SPONSORS

Supporters pay you to post about their items or administrations on the web. Individuals trust proposals more than promotions, so organizations like to work with web-based social networking clients to drive traffic and increment deals. You might be threatened to move toward brands all alone, yet it doesn't damage to connect. For whatever length of time that you can show the scope and estimation of your profiles, you have something worth contributing to a brand and should seek after sponsorship and subsidiary chances. You can't be sure whether you don't attempt!

JOIN AN AFFILIATE PROGRAM

If you've at any point seen somebody on YouTube urge you to "look at the connection in the portrayal," at that point, you're as of now acquainted with subsidiary connections. Organizations offer impacts the opportunity to procure some additional cash by exhibiting their items or administrations, offering an exclusive markdown, and urging watchers to navigate to their page. Web-based life members acquire commission through advancing other brands' items. You don't pay anything to improve, yet you do gain a liberal lump of every deal you drive. For individuals with customized content and a decent specialty, associate promoting is a simple method to adapt to online networking and begin gaining some additional money.

UTILIZING AN AFFILIATE PROGRAM

Finding the correct offshoot program for you is simple on the web. Most member administrations are allowed to join and simply require an application with connections to your web-based life. Insofar as you have a group of people and some pertinent substance, a great many people will have the option to turn into a brand associate with no issue. Take as much time as necessary to inquire about and consider the items you'd prefer to begin offering on your records.

Keep in mind, adapting web-based life doesn't make you a sales rep. Instead, you're in charge of what you advance and how regularly you do as such. Pick items you're glad to utilize yourself and would happily prescribe to anybody. Realness is the way to trust, so stick to what you love, and you'll have the option to transform your web-based social networking accounts into a productive business right away!

THE MOST EFFECTIVE METHOD TO MONETIZE INSTAGRAM

Posting Pictures

On the off chance that you are sure that your photographs are sufficient to be seen and most likely purchased, don't hesitate to uncover them at a bargain. Applications like SnapMyAd empower you to offer your most ideal chances. The more effectively a client puts new pictures, the more supporters will find out about another photographic artist. Appropriately altered photographs will make your substance marked, and individuals will remember you with time. Update hashtags once per week on the off chance that you need to include more endorsers. Answer to the individuals who leave remarks and like your work. Give more consideration to the exchange with guests and not legitimately to deals. Add hashtags to your pictures to stand out and invigorate remarking and talking about. A record that has gathered beyond what 3,000 fans can be viewed as a blog that has a significant effect on the crowd.

Group Promotion

This technique for winning is viewed as one of the quickest and least demanding approaches to begin a business on Instagram without speculations. To bring in cash on a gathering, think of a specific idea and assemble a thought which will be upheld by intrigued endorsers. Probably the most straightforward strategy for advancing your group is remarking on other clients' pics, conventional buying in, exploring your supporters' pictures, and dynamic developing connections. Instagram permits leaving remarks containing links to your record. To turn into an active gathering advertiser, you need the most extreme conceivable number of supporters.

Additionally, you need to refresh substance continually and include new stunning photographs as frequently as could be expected under the circumstances. Right now, the profile will be regularly visited, and the number of preferences will increment just on the off chance that it is intriguing to the intended interest group.

Publicizing Your Products and Services

This sort of salary is useful for planners, picture takers, and other imaginative experts.

If you, as of now, have a record on Instagram with live supporters and their number is more than 100 thousand individuals, it offers you a chance to put advertisements on your posts for a specific charge. For this, your Instagram profile ought to be life, advanced with something like Stormlike's Instagram adherents, and day by day visited by dynamic endorsers. If your record isn't sufficiently famous, you will require a few assets to advance it. You can utilize free techniques, for example, mass-catching and mass-preferring; however, you ought not to anticipate speedy outcomes. You may have fewer supporters. However, you will win less right now. Advancing your chips away at Instagram can not just extend your expert information, pull in more clients, and grow your field of movement, yet additionally gives you helpful suggestions and useful remarks.

Utilizing Instagram as a Tool for Your Own Business

Instagram can be used for a web-based business. On the off chance that you, as of now, have your online store, yet you, despite everything, don't utilize Instagram for publicizing, you should focus on this interpersonal organization. Instagram is never again only online networking for posting individual photographs, yet an extraordinary business device. It will require depictions of your items enthusiastically made by experts, a portrayal offered by the SEO rules, and helpful posting on this interpersonal organization. There are always a couple of individuals among endorsers who will be keen on buying the offered products. Right now, it is a perfect stage for different excellence salons, promoting organizations, shops selling roses and blessings, and so on. A realized record can draw in a genuinely enormous measure of new clients. The advancement of your business profile can be dependent on experts, just as done without anyone else, utilizing both free and paid strategies.

Benefit Using Likes, Subscriptions, and PR

You can advance your record as well as different business profiles. For this, you have to know

all the techniques for advancement, get unique preparation, and regularly improve your aptitudes. There are additionally specific administrations permitting account holders to procure on preferences, memberships, and promotions. The principle pays you can get for publicizing brands and for advancing other clients' records with their items and administrations. Online activities like Userator make it conceivable to get income from making reposts and leaving remarks on the photos you enjoyed.

Master Assessment

It is another choice of adaptation, helpful for open individuals, bloggers, top models, and experts in a specific field of action. For that, the profile ought to have many live supporters. An enormous number of your endorsers may become potential clients of intrigued publicists. The more endorsers, the higher the profit of the page proprietor. It is smarter to consistently search for publicists who will pay you for advancing their items utilizing your record.

HOW TO MONETIZE YOUR FACEBOOK PAGE

There are individuals out there who develop Facebook pages for having them. I've seen handfuls that inside themselves around an idea and grow into something bigger. On the off chance that you have a Facebook page with some degree of following, with or without a site joined, there is a lot of approaches to bring in cash. In all honesty, it's simpler, to begin with, a Facebook page and construct an adapted site than it is to start a website and attempt to assemble a Facebook following from it.

Here are our tips for adapting your Facebook page:

Streamline Your Site for Mobile Devices

Over half of the traffic that peruses Facebook consistently is versatile traffic, which is the reason it is essential to such an extent that if your Facebook connects to an external site that it is enhanced for portable. On the off chance that you can profit by a versatile crowd, you can discover a lot of achievement. Perhaps the ideal approach to guarantee that your traffic from Facebook remains on your site and changes over is to have a responsive website. This implies that regardless of what gadget a client is on your site changes and gives the best client experience.

Sell Digital Content Directly

The main alternative to adapt your Facebook page is the simplest. The least severe case of this is straightforward to portray. Advancing an eBook on your Facebook page is an extraordinary method to keep your crowd drew in and interface over your different sites. On the off chance that you have a lot of substance to disperse, Facebook makes an extraordinary stage of selling your products. Digital books are simple since Amazon and Barnes, and Noble both have dissemination stages which you can exploit, and best of all, Facebook coordinates effectively with the most outside scenes.

Huge brands: Learn how this little skincare startup utilized multi-channel crusades to build perceivability and initiate new devotees significantly.

Send Traffic to Affiliate Marketing Sites

This is another choice you can use to bring in cash by publicizing on Facebook. However, you should be a piece of an associate system. On the off chance that you are powerful, joining a member system ought not to be an issue. Being able to arrive at many individuals is advantageous, and numerous brands will pay heed. When you are a piece of an offshoot organize, merely posting a connection will be sufficient to pick up attribution for your commitment. This is exceptionally simple to set up and use; numerous frameworks have worked in following accessible. Various brands have partners arranges to set up, which they use to deal with their subsidiaries and track the deals or traffic you can drive.

Sell Products through a Facebook App Store

Facebook applications have fallen to some degree over the most recent couple of years. They've been gradually moved further and further down the sidebar, and there's not as much room up top for them as there used to be. This shouldn't imply that you can't at present use them. You should simply set up one of the numerous Facebook business applications. Pick one and use it.

Sell Products through a Website

Precisely the same idea as above can be applied to setting up your customer-facing facade. You have two choices for this; you can either set up a facilitated arrangement, or you can utilize an internet business framework. The last is increasingly costly, however significantly progressively adjustable and better for SEO over the long haul. Advance items and connect your crowd to the item page, that kind of thing. Paid advertisements will help a great deal here because there's not of the room with advancing natural posts.

Advance Products with Exclusive Facebook Offers

In case you're selling items, you can accomplish something other than post "hello, have you see X item? It's cool. You should get it." You can boost traffic and change. You should simply run offers. The natural method for running offers is to advance it on Facebook straightforward. The elective strategy is to utilize the framework of the promotion on Facebook to run suggestions. One may work, or you can use both if you need it.

Sell Products through a Third Party Service

You can structure and offer items without doing any of the article producing, shipping, stock, upkeep, or whatever else. On the off chance that you are inventive, one model is to start putting your craft on different items and selling it. Numerous locales permit you to make effectively print shirts, telephone cases, or socks and sell them. It's straightforward, and it's a course that a great deal of midrange Facebook pages take.

Advance a Local Event with Your Vendor Presence

If your Facebook page is engaged around a geographic area, it will be an incredible open door for you to connect with and acquire outside brands and organizations to engage with your image. You can drive a benefit in a couple of various ways from this. One of them is to set up your very own merchant at the nearby occasion you're advancing so that by improving the time, you're likewise developing yourself. Get more individuals to go to the opening, and more individuals will discover you there, bringing about more deals.

Sell Your Services Growing a Page

So you've grown a Facebook page to its present level, and you're making some measure of progress. Others might want to arrive at that achievement. It's an ideal opportunity to share your abilities. You can sell help where you review a strategy. You can come in and oversee things at a continuous cost on the off chance that you are fruitful there are numerous alternatives to make others effective.

STEP BY STEP INSTRUCTIONS TO MAKE MONEY ON TWITTER

1. Use Sponsored Tweets

Need to bring in cash only for conveying a tweet? You can do that with supported tweets. At the point when you have a strong nearness on Twitter with an enormous after of connected fans, different organizations will pay you to tweet about their items, administrations, or brand. In case you're extremely well known on Twitter, you can just contact brands you love and offer the advantages of elevating their item to your crowd with a paid tweet. On the other hand, various online stages will assist you with interfacing with organizations seeking pay for tweets.

Two or three them are:

- SponsoredTweets: SponsoredTweets is where organizations can look for and associate with Twitter influencers.
- PaidPerTweet: PaidPerTweet lets organizations get to a large number of top Twitter clients, both standard and VIP clients. Costs extend from $1 to $10,000 contingent upon the influencer.

As should be obvious, in case you're a person with a well known Twitter account, you can bring in cash tweeting. Yet additionally, organizations can buy supported tweets from influencers to elevate their business to a different crowd of individuals that need to purchase from you. It's a success win for everybody!

2. Advance Affiliate Products on Twitter

Another approach to adapt your Twitter account is by advancing subsidiary items. At the point when the vast majority consider subsidiary showcasing, they think bloggers arepushing offshoot items on their sites. In any case, you can advance offshoot items on Twitter to bring in cash as well. Member advertising is the way toward developing others' issues. At the point when somebody purchases that item through the connection you shared, you make a commission.

An extraordinary aspect concerning subsidiary advertising is that you can begin as a beginner—you don't have to have a tremendous Twitter following to be acknowledged into offshoot promoting programs. To discover partner items, you can advance on Twitter, make a record on a subsidiary showcasing system like:

- ShareASale

- Amazon Associates

- FlexOffers

- ClickBank

Try not to push any partner item you run over, however. If you advance a considerable amount of various issues with no justifiable purpose, your Twitter profile won't be engaged, and your intended interest group won't realize what they're getting from every day to the following.

Simply investigate the entirety of the various sorts of subsidiary items you can discover on ClickBank. To be fruitful at partner promoting, it's insightful to pick a specialty. Pick a hobby that you're educated about and that you're enthusiastic about as well. For example, a nourishment blogger should stay with cooking, nourishment, and wine items since they realize that their crowd is keen on those sorts of things. Furthermore, their group will confide in their proposals in the classification and be bound to purchase. Try not to spam your devotees with subsidiary connections, either. Blend them in with your ordinary substance, so you don't annoy your devotees. An excessive number of suspicious links can get your record suspended as well.

3. Advance Your Products

On the off chance that you sell your items, an extraordinary method to bring in cash on Twitter is by elevating them to your supporters. Since your adherents are as of now tailing you, they're probably going to be keen on the items you offer. In case you're thinking about how to advance a question on Twitter, it's very straightforward—simply share a post.In certainty, as indicated by considers, Twitter clients shopped online 6.9 times each month, while non-clients shopped online only 4.3 times each month. Additionally, Twitter clients intended to burn through 21.7% more than non-clients in a multi-month timespan.

4. Produce Traffic for Your Website

Regardless of whether your business doesn't sell items, you can, in any case, use Twitter to produce traffic for your site or create more leads for an assistance based business. For example, Ali Marten, proprietor of the well-known nourishment blog Gimme Some Oven, shared this post on Twitter to tell her adherents about the most recent formula on her webpage. Sharing your most recent blog entries on Twitter will enable more clients to find your site, help your site traffic, and become your blogging profession.

You can even be proactive about creating traffic and leads via scanning for necessary strings and conversations on Twitter.NOnaccount of help based efficient a dental specialist's office, you could scan Twitter for watchwords like "searching for dental specialists" or "dental specialists in [your city]." When you discover tweets from individuals that are searching for dental specialists, fire up a discussion. Answer to their tweet by saying something like, "Hello Sarah, I see that you're searching for dental specialists in the territory... " and leave a connection to your business site.

5. Fabricate an Email List

Building an email list is probably the ideal approaches to produce more deals for your business. With email advertising, you can message your supporters straightforwardly to share organization news or your most recent blog entries, declare new items, advance glimmer deals, and the sky is the limit from there.

As per WPForms, mechanized messages can support income by as much as 320%. To fabricate an email list, make a leave purpose popup utilizing OptinMonster to catch the eye of your site guests before they leave your site. Offering a lead magnet, which is a complimentary gift like a guide, schedule, digital book, or layout, in return for your guests' email addresses, is an extraordinary method to develop your email list rapidly. Be that as it may, how would you build your email list on Twitter?

It's simple! You should simply share your lead magnet on Twitter alongside a connect to your email list opt-in greeting page. With this procedure for bringing in cash on Twitter, you can transform your Twitter supporters into endorsers and afterward into clients with focused email showcasing efforts.

6. Give Customer Service

Giving quality client support is critical to any active business. While providing client care doesn't assist you with bringing in cash legitimately, it can help you with creating more leads and keep your current clients. Indeed, as indicated by HelpScout, 7 out of 10 U.S. buyers state they've gone through more cash to work with an organization that conveys extraordinary help. Also, today, buyers need snappier and more advantageous client care than any other time in recent memory. Which is the reason you ought to utilize Twitter to give client support?

Some large organizations like UPS have whole Twitter accounts devoted to client assistance. You don't need to claim a significant organization to give excellent client care on Twitter. You should simply be accessible to your clients and assist them with unraveling their issues in a convenient way—which will enable your business to drive more deals. In any case, being there for your clients every minute of every day is almost conceivable, except ifyou utilize a Twitter chatbot. A Twitter chatbot can be accessible for your clients day and night and utilizations human-made consciousness (AI) to address client questions.

For example, look at how Patron Tequila can bring in cash with a Twitter bot. Right now, chatbot prescribes various things the client should purchase for their extraordinary occasion. It resembles the client has their one of a kind individual customer. Building a Twitter chatbot appears to be troublesome; however, don't stress. You can utilize an instrument like ManyChat to handily make a Twitter bot for your business.

7. Run a Giveaway

Running a giveaway appears to be an extraordinary method to advance your business and construct brand mindfulness; however, does it truly assist you with bringing in cash? You're in karma, it indeed does!

Need verification? KnivesShipFree.com, an eCommerce store selling premium blades, utilized a giveaway to transform window-customers into clients and created over $10,000 in deals. Along these lines, if you need to bring in cash on Twitter, take a stab at running a giveaway.

You can utilize an instrument like RafflePress, which is one of the most impressive giveaway modules available, to fabricate and deal with your giveaway effortlessly. With RafflePress, you can make a giveaway point of arrival in a matter of moments utilizing their intuitive giveaway manufacturer (and there's a FREE form). Another incredible thing about RafflePress is itsextra checked activities. Extra activities give clients additional passages for finishing explicit errands, such as visiting a page on your site, tailing you on Twitter, joining your email rundown, and substantially more.

Thus, by running your giveaway with RafflePress, you can create more deals and develop your Twitter following simultaneously.

8. Make Twitter Ads

Another approach to producing more sales for your business is by making Twitter Ads. Twitter Ads will enable your business to contact more individuals on the web—your present adherents, however different clients on Twitter as well. The more individuals that know about your business, the more deals you can make. Twitter Ads look merely like various tweets in the channel; however,they are unmistakably marked "advanced" like in the model underneath.

Twitter Ads are so viable because you're ready to demonstrate your promotion to the perfect individuals. You can show your Twitter Ad to clients dependent on their particular advantages, socioeconomics, and even their movement on Twitter. By utilizing focused on Twitter Ads, you can elevate your business to vast amounts of clients that are keen on precisely what you're advertising.

Along these lines, when a client sees your Twitter Ad in their channel and thinks "Goodness, that is exactly what I required!", they'll be bound to tap on your Ad and make a buy.

9. Adapt Your Twitter Presence

On YouTube, makers can adapt their channels, which lets them place advertisements in their recordings and live streams. At the point when a promotion is watched or clicked, the maker brings in cash from those publicists. Furthermore, You can do that on Twitter, as well! A couple of years prior, Twitter revealed the Twitter Media Studio, which lets content makers adapt their quality on Twitter.

Twitter Media Studio lets you place in-stream video promotions and in-stream video sponsorships directly into your image safe Twitter video content with the goal that you can procure cash legitimately from the stage. Different highlights of Twitter Media Studio include:

- Producer – Broadcast proficient live streams, advance and timetable live streams, and make moment features of your flow with LiveCut.

- Library – Manage the entirety of your recordings, pictures, and GIFs in one spot. You can likewise include client jobs and consents over your group.

- Analytics – Measure your presentation on Twitter by survey measurements of your tweets and profit from adapted recordings.

Presto! Presently you realize how to adapt Twitter and drive more deals for your business utilizing one of the most well-known web-based life stages.

STEP BY STEP INSTRUCTIONS TO MONETIZE YOUR YOUTUBE

One energizing approach to support your pay is to begin bringing in cash on YouTube. Individuals love recordings and offer them over a wide range of web-based life stages. Simply consider the last time you looked over Facebook and what number of records there are present! On the off chance that you can figure out how to adapt YouTube for your undertakings, you'll indeed have something going for you.

Why YouTube?

The slick thing about YouTube is that it's video-based, which for some, individuals can be an interesting approach to bring in cash. YouTube is free, it's genuinely open regardless of whether you don't have extravagant hardware, and it has a large number of clients. A lot of individuals get looking great so far, utilizing just their cell phone as a video recording gadget. Transferring your recordings is genuinely necessary — it requires a free record, and that is it. You'll have to have your record set ready for adapting — yet the procedure is straightforward. You can learn increasingly here about how to get that going.

How Might I Monetize YouTube?

YouTube is an exciting approach to bring in cash, and when it's done well, it tends to be exceptionally rewarding. In the case of nothing else, it's certainly worth a more intensive hope to check whether it'd be a solid match for you. We should look at it!

1. First of all: AdSense

YouTube will be putting advertisements on your recordings regardless, so you should gain by them by getting your AdSense set up once you hit 1,000 supporters and 4,000 watch hours inside a year on your Channel. (You can get your channel arranged while you hold on to arrive at those measurements.) This is done inside your YouTube account. You may likewise need to look into what sorts of recordings will meet all requirements for Adsense income.

2. Fill Your Funnels

On the off chance that you as of now have a set up online business with email select ins as well as items available to be purchased, YouTube can be an extraordinary method to fill your business pipe. Utilize your recordings to give accommodating, helpful substance to your perusers and watchers, and in the video point to your select in (or make a unique new pick in only for your watchers). When somebody enters their email address, you can send a progression of messages assembling your relationship with them and, in the long run offering your items or administrations available to be purchased.

I have found YouTube an extraordinary method to assemble my email list. The approaching traffic as of now changes over at a lot higher rate than my other internet based life channels. Furthermore, on the off chance that you have a blog, make recordings around a portion of your adapted presents and connection on them inside your video depiction.

3. Associate Marketing

The ideal approach to prevail with associate showcasing is to share the truth about how your item transformed you. YouTube is a GREAT spot to begin sharing — you can show how you utilize the question, why you love it, answer reasonable inquiries, and that's just the beginning. (Simply be sure you follow any of your organization's consistent rules!)

The video takes into account some new approaches to the interface that aren't depicted continuously well in content. You can do "unpacking" recordings, instructional exercises, item audits, and "takes." Include your subsidiary connection inside the video portrayal or potentially inside the video. Remember to reveal!

4. Adapt YouTube with Brand Sponsors

Similar waymarks are working with bloggers for sponsorship openings; they're searching for extraordinary YouTubers to share their items far and wide. Start pitching organizations you love with sponsorship openings and see what winds up working for you! Simply make sure to follow great sponsorship rules — just work with brands you trust to advance items you put stock in and are essential to your watchers. You will likewise need to uncover this relationship appropriately. Google has paid item arrangement rules, which were refreshed on December 5, 2018.

5. Adapt Your Channel with Community Sponsors

For some time now, YouTube has made accessible a "Support" button on some gaming channels. They just began beta testing the alternative with non-gaming channels also. For $4.99 every month, your greatest fans can Sponsor your channel. This will give them a little identification that shows by their name in your remarks. You can likewise offer them unique advantages like support just substance. Makers get 70% of the income after nearby deals charge is deducted.

To check whether you have this choice accessible, head over to Channel > Status and Features > Sponsorships.

6. Become an Amazon Influencer

Amazon, as of late, presented its Influencer program which permits online networking influencers on YouTube, Facebook, Instagram and Twitter to procure cash through their Amazon proposals. When affirmed, you will be able to make a page on Amazon loaded up with items you suggest, similar to this one. You can then simply share the customized connect on your online life channels. At the point when somebody navigates and gets, you will win a commission on endorsed item classes. Reward: Influencers can likewise connect to their page inside messages! Something not offered to customary Amazon Associates.

This program isn't available to everybody. On the off chance that you apply with your Twitter or YouTube account, you ought to get a prompt acknowledgment or decrease. Facebook and Instagram are considered by hand.

7. Advantage from YouTube Red Subscribers

YouTube Red is a membership administration that clients can purchase that kills advertisements from their recordings. As a YouTube Creator, you can begin getting a commission dependent on how much time Red endorsers are spending on your records. You will have the option to see your YouTube Red watch time in your Analytics.

To expand your income, ensure your recordings are intriguing and valuable, with extraordinary SEO, to catch however many eyeballs as could be expected under the circumstances and keep them returning for additional. You won't be endorsed to get Red salary until you satisfy the guideline adaptation prerequisites (1,000 supporters and 4,000 watch hours in the earlier year time frame).

8. Sell Merch

Ifyour divertgenuinely takes off and builds up its very own existence — or if the brand you're building does — you can make and sell the uniquely marked products in your recordings. Shirts, mugs, canvas packs, and things like that can be excellent merchandise choices, and there are a few distinctive drop-shippers accessible so you won't even necessarily need to disturb stock. This can be particularly acceptable if your image has a great deal of fun. This is another chance to utilize that Amazon Influencer interface.

Continuously Disclose

Much the same as with blogging, you have to make explicit revelations in your YouTube recordings when you're advancing supported, or subsidiary repaid content. Not doing so places you infringing upon the FTC, the YouTube stage rules, or both. You can peruse up additional on YouTube's revelation necessities here so you can remain on target.

CONCLUSIONS
THE FUTURE OF SOCIAL MEDIA

Online life advances quicker than the promoting business can keep up. With calculation changes, new bleeding edge highlights, and a consistent stream of updates, it very well may be hard to know the most recent social patterns. In any case, that doesn't mean it's challenging to remain up to date. "It takes work to keep steady over all the changes," said Chelsea McDonald, senior web-based life strategist at DEG Digital. "The patterns are only that for an explanation; it's what's famous and happening at this moment, which was not well known two weeks prior and will be dead two months from now."

Anyway, troublesome, it's essential to focus on creative patterns and foresee the ones to come. This will keep your business severe and set you apart from different organizations, regardless of what stages you're on. For instance, Facebook is the quickest developing internet based life organization since it "is by all accounts driving the route with web-based life's future," said web-based life pro and independent author Lindsay Patton-Carson.

"Since its creation, Facebook has procured 79 organizations, most broadly Instagram and WhatsApp, transforming it into internet-based life's greatest aggregate," she included. "It will be fascinating to check whether different stages consider their own M&As." It is safe to say that you are set up for what web based life has coming up for what's to come?

Online networking is continually advancing, and it's energizing to consider what it will resemble in only a couple of years. This implies the universe of Social Media Monitoring needs to stay aware of the requests of internet-based life clients as brands keep on adjusting their systems once new patterns develop. So what will the eventual fate of internet-based life look like from a client, brand, and Social Media Monitoring point of view? How about we investigate the numerous potential patterns we could be seeing when one year from now.

What will web-based life resemble?

1. More protection and security:

In the present atmosphere of web-based life, it's a higher priority than at any other time for brands to discover and execute techniques for building customer trust. This starts with how they associate with crowds. Protection concerns are on the ascent as internet based life clients are getting substantially more mindful of how their information is being utilized. Along these lines, the eventual fate of online networking will see an expansion in clients selecting what's known as "Dull Social." This includes any online social collaboration that happens secretly, for instance, informing applications, email, and different outlets for private sharing. 84% of purchasers' outbound sharing from sites currently happens through private, Dark Social channels, for example, these, and we will hope to see this expansion in the following hardly any years.

2. More video:

Its a well known fact that video utilization through internet-based life is on the ascent. It's evaluated that individuals take a gander at recordings multiple times longer than inactive substances, for example, content and pictures, on both Facebook and Instagram. Along these lines, it's nearly ensured that we will see considerably more recordings all over web-based life later on, including live recordings, which have increased a lot of fame as of late.

3. Less close to home substance, yet more images:

Facebook claims that they recorded a 21% drop in unique, individual updates in 2016 as clients are currently imparting in shared articles and pictures alone. Web-based social networking clients, as a rule, are sharing less close to home data on significant systems and want to exhibit outside substance, for example, an exciting video or an original image they ran over to their companions.

4. Premium administrations and less promotions:

Promotions have been the plague of online networking for quite a while now, and web-based life clients are beginning to get tired. Be that as it may, numerous individuals have been happy to forfeit adless encounters for nothing, advertisement immersed ones. Premium administrations could be on the ascent as online networking clients will, in general, favor excellent pictures, recordings, and sound as that is the thing that they have gotten familiar with as of late. In any case, the truth will surface eventually if they are eager to burn through cash on it.

5. Portable centered encounters:

The eventual fate of online life is portable. An expected 3 billion individuals will approach cell phones by 2020. Furthermore, an ever-increasing number of individuals are utilizing their cell phones as their primary hotspot for getting to social stages. That is the reason future steps will be planned considering cell phones from the beginning.

6. Less composing:

As indicated by Andrew Ng, the Chief Scientist at Baidu, in any event, half of the online hunts will be brought out through pictures and voice by 2020. With the ever-expanding prominence of voice and image search just as sound bit messages, online networking could see the demonstration of composing become outdated later on.

7. More visuals:

With the fame of web-based life stages, for example, Instagram and Snapchat, we are now beginning to see a monstrous increment in visual-based substance. Since camera gets to is such a lot simpler now than it was a couple of years back, as virtually every telephone has a worked in the camera, photographs and recordings will keep on immersing online networking. Jay Singh, CEO of PHL Venture Company, takes note of the significance of the camera:

"We keep on observing a move toward a live substance that is formed through a camera. The camera continues developing insignificance, and the capacity to see through others' focal points progressively is turning into an amazing power in online networking."

8. A.R. what's more, V.R's. impact has just barely started:

In the following couple of years, the universe of showcasing will present increasingly functional utilizations of Virtual Reality (V.R.) and Augmented Reality (A.R.). A similar will apply to web-based social networking stages. As per Hootsuite, social informing applications Facebook Messenger, WhatsApp, Instagram,

Snapchat, Bitmoji, WeChat, and QQ will utilize A.R. to help promoting income sooner rather than later. Innovation is one of the quickest developing businesses around today, and A.R., what's more, V.R. is no particular case.

By what means will brands adjust to the eventual fate of online life?

1. Knowing their crowd:

As opposed to barraging them with advertisements, which keeps on disappointing numerous web-based life clients, brands must associate with their groups on an increasingly important level by treating them like people as opposed to a mass wellspring of income. Purchasers are thus bound to believe that brand once that technique for correspondence is built up. What's more, the more brands think about their crowd, the simpler it is for them to focus on their informing to each portion.

2. Making shareable substance:

Since web-based life, clients are beginning to avoid sharing exclusive updates freely on the web and selecting to share content they find online with their companions;instead, brands need to give that substance to them. Regardless of whether that is an inspiring story or an amusing video, brands need to move their crowd somehow or another so they draw in with their image just as urge them to impart that substance to their companions.

3. Grasping visual and innovation:

The fate of web-based life will transcendently be comprised of pictures and recordings, so marks truly need to bounce on that fleeting trend on the off chance that they are going to keep up. A.R. also, V.R. is quick turning into an indispensable piece of many promoting efforts, so marks additionally need to see approaches to join these advancements into their advertising efforts.

By what method will Social Media Monitoring be influenced?

Because of the way that protection and security among web-based life clients are holding much more weight in the present atmosphere, Social Media Monitoring and Social Listening will be influenced as clients adjust their protection settings. It's so significant for brands and Social Media Monitoring organizations to pay attention to clients' interests and do all that they can to guarantee that they feel ensured and that their trust won't be abused or misused.

Online networking Monitoring will likewise need to pay attention to visual notices very. With regards to marking logos inside shared pictures and recordings, brands need an approach to screen and measure that information, just as the printed opinions of that brand. That is the reason a logo identification instrument is imperative for Social Media Monitoring organizations to give to their clients.

Along these lines, there you have it. These are only a portion of the web-based life patterns we will hope to see inside the following scarcely any years. Web-based life will experience a few changes, however, generally, a large number of these patterns have been anticipated as we've been seeing them unfurl continuously. All in all, what do you figure the eventual fate of web-based social networking will have coming up?

Printed in Poland
by Amazon Fulfillment
Poland Sp. z o.o., Wrocław

56078409R00101